Agility... P9-EDO-722

is
fun!

Book 2

Control & handling techniques
for competitors at all levels of agility

by Ruth Hobday

Photographs by Sandra Russell
(Russell Fine Art).

Pedigree
Petfoods
Division of Mars G.B. Limited

Supported by Pedigree Petfoods,
the makers of Pedigree Chum.

THE OUR DOGS PUBLISHING COMPANY LTD

OGS PUBLISHING CO. LTD.,
Oxford Road Station Approach, Manchester M60 1SX

Telephone: 061 236 2660
Fax: 061 236 5534

Ruth Hobday, Willow Batch, Carding Mill Valley,
Church Stretton, Shropshire. Telephone: 0694 723126

All photographs by Sandra Russell of RUSSELL FINE ART (& OUR DOGS'
Staff Photographer), 33, Sycamore Road, Eccles, Manchester M30 8LH.
Telephone: 061 789 4819.

The author and publishers gratefully acknowledge the help and assistance of the following
in the production of this book.
John Coleman, for his contribution on the chapter on obstacle building.
Dawn McConnell, illustrations.
Jackie Manley, typesetting.
Peter Embling, editing, design and production.
Vince Hogan, Managing Director of The Our Dogs Publishing Co. Ltd.
Also thanks to all the handlers and their dogs who acted as models for the photographs.

First Published 1992.
The 'Our Dogs' Publishing Company Limited.
ISBN 0 903034 12 3

The Our Dogs Publishing Company Limited
Typeset at Our Dogs.

Printed by Y. C. G. Ltd., Wakefield, West Yorkshire.

ABOUT RUTH HOBDAY

From an early age at school Ruth was involved in competitive sports— especially athletics. She had always wanted a dog but her first, a Cocker Spaniel called Rusty, didn't do very well at obedience classes!

Moving to Shropshire she then acquired a cross breed, Kim, and Sheba, a small and rather nervous Shetland Sheepdog. As Sheba kept breaking stays, Ruth turned to Kim, the cross breed, who in 1970-71 began to impress winning at Beginners & Novice classes. By 1980 Ruth with Riki, also a Sheltie, 'discovered' the world of Agility and enjoyed its more exciting atmosphere.

In 1986 Riki and Border Collie 'Kwippy' were eclipsed by 'Heidi' now so well known as the Agility Dog of the Year in 1987 and 1988.

Ruth started obedience instruction in the late 60's and instructed at Shrewsbury Dog Training Club for about fifteen years. In 1981 Shrewsbury began Agility and Ruth became their instructor, later joined by Jo Evason. She has also run her own local obedience class for the last 12 years.

Ruth has now given up her career in teaching and has become a full time Agility trainer since 1987 having built a whole new set of equipment from scratch and has been running the 'Hurricane Dog Training Centre' in Shropshire since April 1988.

In 1991 Ruth accepted an invitation to give two 4 day courses in America, one in Dallas the other in Detroit. These were a great success and gave an indication of the following Agility has in the United States. Many copies of Agility is Fun (Book 1) have been sold on that side of the Atlantic.

Back home Agility is Fun became available in video form and a reference to the videos is made elsewhere in this book. Another video is planned showing the progress of puppies from 6-18 months.

Whilst 'Heidi' has had time off to have puppies, Ruth has been kept busy on the circuit with 'Susie'. Ruth has now selected two puppies from Heidi's litter for training.

ACKNOWLEDGEMENTS

Jo Evason who checked the control exercises.

John Coleman for his work on Chapter 15.

Val Mackay for her continued help and encouragement.

HURRICANE DOG TRAINING AGILITY COURSES

WEEKEND AND MID-WEEK

Individual attention at all levels of ability. Full set of equipment including Dog Cross and Wishing Well, also Mini equipment.

COURSES CAN ALSO BE ARRANGED AT YOUR OWN CLUB.

ON-SITE ACCOMODATION AVAILABLE.

Details : Ruth Hobday
Willow Batch, Carding Mill Valley, Church Stretton, Shropshire. SY6 6JG.
Tel: 0694 723126

2 VIDEOS NOW AVAILABLE FROM RUTH HOBDAY:
Agility is Fun & Agility is Fun, Control Exercises.
Agility is Fun (Book 1) available from OUR DOGS.

CONTENTS

Chapter	Page
Introduction	1
1 What makes a winner?	5
2 The agility show	7
3 Mini agility	13
4 Your first show	17
5 Walking the course	31
6 Warm up exercises	37
7 Jumping exercises	41
8 Obstacle training	65
9 Obstacle training using tunnels and the tyre	113
10 Obstacle training with the long jump and the table	135
11 Exercises using the weaving poles	147
12 Obstacle awareness exercises	155
13 Problems	159
14 Problem dogs	187
15 Obstacle building	195
Conclusion	207

Riki (Lythwood Sealord CDEX),
to whose memory this book is dedicated.

INTRODUCTION

Since completing the first book, *Agility is Fun*, I have been delighted by a continuing stream of letters of appreciation, including a great many from overseas. There has been an overwhelming response to the control exercises at the back of the book which the majority seemed to find particularly valuable.

A great many readers also wrote asking for help with agility problems, or enrolled for my agility courses.

Book 2 greatly extends the control exercises and includes a section dealing with some of the more common problems that arise in agility training.

Also, by popular request, there is a chapter on the construction of my adjustable contact equipment.

The first book dealt with teaching the beginner dog the basics of agility. Book 2 seeks to take the handler on into the world of competition for both mini and standard size dogs.

Book 2 covers completely new ground and I hope you will find it as useful as *Agility is Fun*, (Book 1).

AGILITY
THE GOOD OLD DAYS?

This article by Ruth Hobday was originally published in the OUR DOGS Annual 1989.

Agility is now 10 years old. How has the sport changed in 10 years? Has it changed for the better? What does the future hold? What will agility be like in another 10 years? These are questions that are often asked.

I'm not sure of the answers to these questions but one thing I do know from experience, is that the agility show of today is very different from the agility show of 10 years ago. I was just starting out in the sport then and I have many memories of those early shows.

One of the biggest problems then was finding out where and when there was a competition. To begin with there were very few clubs who did agility training let alone thought about running an open competition. One or two Obedience Shows held an agility fun class and Pedigree Petfoods ran the first Olympia Qualifiers, but I think the most important contribution to the start of agility shows was made by the late Ted Groome who had a full set of agility equipment and took it from show to show, where he organised agility classes.

I went to as many of these shows as I could find out about. They were held mainly in the South of England and with no 'Agility Voice' advertising tended to be by word of mouth and not very reliable.

Even when you knew of a competition, finding the venue often proved difficult with only the odd dog show sign to help you.

However, once found these early agility shows were great fun and I made many new friends, some of whom I still meet at shows today.

After finding the venue, parking the car and giving the dogs a run, it was time to find the ring. Then usually around 10 am we made a leisurely start. First helping to put the equipment out, then finding the club secretary and paying our entry money. At these early shows you paid on the day, usually 50p and often you could have more than one go. It was quite common for handlers to do two rounds on the same course with either only the best round being counted, or both scores being added together.

The equipment up and entries taken, it was time to walk the course. At the first few shows that I went to, you were allowed to walk the course with your dog and I can vividly remember the first time a parallel spread was used. There was a lot of discussion, handlers got down on hands and knees to view this from dogs level, then someone hit on the idea of picking the dog up and showing it the back pole, soon everyone was doing this. Dogs were also shown the correct hole to jump through at the tyre.

After we'd walked the course came the briefing, not very brief in those days and open to quite a bit of discussion, but all very friendly.

Then came the draw. This consisted of Ted placing small boards face down on the ground numbered 1 to however many competitors there were, remember 30 was a very large entry then. Everyone chose a board and apprehensively turned it over dreading to find the number 1 on it. I remember that we all kept obediently to our running order although there were no ring callers in those days.

The draw completed, the judge then proceeded to position his stewards. Not just jump stewards for at the start of agility shows a steward judged each contact point while the judge stood in the middle of the ring and counted how many times the stewards put a hand up.

With the stewards and time keeper in position, the first dog got ready to begin his round.

The other competitors and any spectators sat around the ring watching and I'm sure I remember the sun shining a lot more than it does these days.

What were those early courses like? How did the dogs do?

To begin with courses tended to be very simple, a figure of eight starting and finishing on the table being the most common. It was the obstacles themselves that caused most problems. Very few handlers had access to equipment for training and often the first time a dog met a tunnel, tyre or piece of contact equipment, was in the ring. Elimination by getting 3 refusals was very common and also a lot of dogs ran out of the ring either to husbands or wives, or just to have a nose at other dogs. Few dogs seemed able to really concentrate on the round although they certainly had fun and were very entertaining to watch.

The equipment itself caused several problems for the judge. Weaving poles were usually broomsticks with nails in the bottoms stuck into the ground and these often needed straightening after each dog. Faults in the poles were not marked but they had to be completed correctly and often took quite a time. There were very few fast weaving dogs in those days.

Tunnels are now safely staked.

Tunnels were not staked down and it was not uncommon for a dog to get tangled up and have to be helped out, or to move the base of the tunnel as he went through.

Contact points were not painted a different colour, but just marked by a line and were very difficult to judge. To begin with the up contact was not marked only the down. Dogs were particularly good at missing the contact on the 'A' frame often leaping off way above it. Its a wonder they didn't injure themselves.

With 10 faults for a refusal, not 5 as now, and with the inexperience of handlers and dogs many came out of the ring with cricket scores. In fact not getting the dreaded E was a real achievement and was greeted by a round of hearty applause. However, elimination didn't mean you had to leave the ring, you were encouraged to continue. Also with such a small class the judge had time to talk to each competitor and advise on future training.

After the competition was finished handlers were allowed to practise on the equipment. Everyone was keen to do this because often it was their only chance to use agility equipment but it was very dangerous with several fights occurring and things like two dogs meeting on top of the dog walk commonplace.

Around this time the first Pedigree Chum Olympia heats were held at some of the big agricultural shows. There were about 5 heats and the course which had no contact equipment in, was exactly the same for each heat, enabling the lucky few with access to equipment, to build a similar course and practise.

At these heats we first met electronic timing and the most common way of getting your dog to go ahead through the finish was to throw your lead, which you were allowed to carry in your hand. I also remember one dog that always competed with a dumbbell in his mouth.

So how are shows different today?

Firstly there is now a vast choice of shows so that you can almost do a show every week and still not go to them all. "Agility Voice", the official magazine of the Agility Club gives details of shows and venues.

Entries now cost £1.00 or £1.50 and have to be in 2 or 3 weeks before the show.

There is however, more choice of classes with both agility and jumping (no contacts) classes, also pairs, teams and gamblers etc. Dogs are now classified as Starters, Novice or Senior depending upon what they have won. There are also separate classes for mini dogs under 15" and classes for junior handlers only.

Finding the venue is usually easier with most clubs putting 'agility' signs out on the roads.

Early starts, 9.00 am judging, are usual and necessary with very large classes. There were 408 dogs entered in the Pedigree Chum heat at Rugby in 1991.

Upon arrival at the show you first collect your ring number which usually has your running order for each class already written on the back. There will be two or more rings, so several classes go on at the same time. Ring callers are essential and running orders have to be kept to so that the class keeps flowing, even so 7.0 and 8.0 pm finishes are not unusual.

Dogs are not now allowed to walk the course with you, there is no practising before or after in the ring and handlers must not carry anything in their hands.

Its 5 faults for everything now, the weaving poles are marked and all contact points count. Competition is very keen and often now a clear round, even a fast one, may not win you a rosette. Some clubs do give clear round rosettes to encourage the not so fast but accurate dog.

Now if you get eliminated you may not be able to finish the round and we've even had classes when a standard of 10 or 15 faults has applied.

Oh, for the good old days you might say, but are you sure?

Certainly when I crawl out of bed in the dark early hours, have a long drive before an 8.30 am briefing and then find I'm not drawn to run until number 285, I may think back longingly to those early days but I'm sure agility is a better sport now. The dogs are fitter and far better controlled, even the beginner dog rarely runs out of the ring. The equipment is definitely better and much safer, courses are more interesting and judging is an art competently carried out by the majority of today's judges.

As in all things there is room for improvement, especially in the organisation of such large classes and thought is needed on how to encourage those competitors with slower accurate dogs.

However, one thing that I feel hasn't changed and I hope never will, is the friendship and fun that you find at agility shows. So if you haven't been bitten by the agility bug yet, why not have a go!

1
WHAT MAKES A WINNER?

Many people dream of having a really good winning agility dog. Some are lucky enough to get one and do really well and a few handlers seem to have several good dogs. Many dogs, however, will always be also-rans and never win any major prizes.

So what's the secret? What makes a dog a winner?

Does the dog need to be bred especially for agility? There are many rescue dogs that do really well so obviously the answer to that one is 'No'.

The dog must be physically sound but apart from that I don't feel that breeding is particular important in agility.

I think for a dog to have the chance of becoming a top flight agility winner he needs the following:

Fitness and stamina. The top dogs are as lively and keen at the end of a day's competitions as at the beginning and can do six or seven rounds in a knockout without tiring.

The type of exercise the dog gets, apart from agility training, is very important. To

Knowing your dog has tried his best, this is what its all about.

5

build hard muscle he needs road work as well as free running.

Instant response to the handler and very quick reactions. In agility everything happens so quickly that the dog must respond instantly without stopping to think about it. The handler needs pretty fast reactions too.

A love of agility. The top agility dogs obviously love their agility and once in the ring are oblivious to anything but the job in hand

Add to these three a good slice of luck and you should have your dream dog.

However, agility is not all about winning, although it is very nice to win and everyone likes to get rosettes. As much as I like to win, to me the joy of agility is getting the best out of my dog and both of us enjoying it. To come out of the ring knowing your dog has done all that you asked and tried his very best gives a real sense of achievement even if a rosette is not the end product.

Most agility people have their dogs firstly as pets and secondly as competition dogs and that's the way it should be. So accept your dog's limitations and work towards getting the very best from each dog. Be fair to the dog, be consistent and don't ask too much and make sure he understands what you want.

Finally and most important, keep it fun.

2

THE AGILITY SHOW

So you've decided to go to an Agility Show. What sort of classes are there and which can you enter? The show schedule will set out all the classes at that particular show and give the restrictions on entry to each class.

The Kennel Club classification must be used for all agility shows in this country and is as follows:

Classes may be scheduled for Agility Tests, as Agility classes or jumping classes. Agility classes to include contact points and jumping classes where there are no contact obstacles. With this proviso classes are defined as follows:

CLASSES

Elementary
For owners, handlers or dogs which have not gained a third prize or above in an Agility and/or a Jumping Class at a licensed Agility Test.

Starters
For dogs which have not won an Agility and/or Jumping Class at a licensed Agility Test (Elementary excepted).

Novice
For dogs which have not won a total of two first prizes in Novice, Intermediate, Senior, Advanced or Open at a licensed Agility Test.

Intermediate
Open to all except dogs eligible for Elementary and Starters Classes at a licensed Agility Test.

Seniors
Open to dogs having won at least two first prizes at a licensed Agility Test (Elementary and Starter wins excepted).

Advanced
Open to dogs having a minimum of four wins at a licensed Agility Test, two of which must be gained in Senior or Open Agility Classes (Elementary and Starter wins excepted).

Open
Open to all.

NOVELTY CLASSES

Is the general heading for classes, which are other than standard agility or jumping e.g. Team Events, Gamblers, Snooker, Pairs, Knock-Out, Two-Dog Relays, Time Gamble or other non-standard classes as defined in a show schedule.

Entry Eligibility. All wins in Standard Agility or Jumping Classes should be added together and counted up to and including the seventh day before the date of closing entries. Only wins in Standard Classes count, not those in Novelty Classes.

Some Novelty Classes need more explanation as many beginner handlers are put off having a go in what can be very enjoyable classes.

Gamblers. The dog is given a set time (usually 35-50 seconds) to accumulate points on the course which normally contains the three pieces of contact equipment. Usually each obstacle can be done in any order, a maximum of twice correctly, and points are given for each obstacle completed correctly. Contacts and weaving poles are normally worth 3 (or 30) points. Tyres, long jump, tunnels, spreads and the well are normally worth 2 (or 20) points and single hurdles are worth 1 (or 10) points but the judge is at liberty to alter this if he wishes.

When the allotted time is up, a whistle is blown and usually the dog has a further 10-15 seconds to attempt the joker. This will be some combination of obstacles at the judge's discretion which, if done successfully in the time, will add to the dog's score.

There are various restrictions a judge may choose to impose on a gambler's course and the judge's briefing is very important before planning your course.

Take your own line. This is usually a full agility course with the first and last obstacles decided by the judge. The handler has to work out the best course to take doing each obstacle once only. Faults are incurred as normal.

Snooker.

A maximum time is set by the judge during which the dog completes the obstacles in normal Snooker order.

The higher value obstacles are the harder ones, with the black normally being a piece of contact equipment.

The winner is the dog with the highest score, the dog's time being used to separate equal scores.

Pairs and Two-Dog Relays.

Pairs can be jumping or agility or a combination of the two.

Often there is a baton change and the time is a combined one of the two dogs.

Sometimes both dogs do the same course; other times one dog does half and the other finishes the course.

Pairs Pursuit.

This is an interesting competition. It is a knock-out, with each pair consisting of a jumping dog and an agility dog. One pair's jumping dog completes a jumping course, normally around the edge of the ring. At the same time the opposite pair's agility dog collects points on an agility course, usually set in the centre of the ring. This agility dog has the amount of time it takes the opposing jumping dog to get round.

When both pairs have run, the pair with the agility dog having the most points goes through to the next round.

Knock-Outs.

This can be for individuals or pairs. All the dogs taking part go into a draw which determines when they run. Each winning dog goes through to the next round until two dogs or pairs run off in the final.

Time-Gamble.

This is normally an agility course with standard marking, but time faults are added for being either over or under the course time set by the judge.

Time and Score.

Usually a jumping class. The dog scores a point for each obstacle done correctly over a course set by the judge. Upon completion of the course the dog continues round again until the end of the time given. The dog getting most points is the winner.

Time, Fault and Out.

This is similar to Time and Score but the dog is eliminated as soon as he makes a mistake.

QUALIFYING EVENTS.

As you get more and more interested in agility showing you will begin to enter the qualifying heats for the big competitions sponsored by some of the large firms. Most of these are open to all and there is nothing to stop a beginner having a go. So what is on offer?

PEDIGREE PETFOODS sponsors five big competitions:

The Pedigree Chum Agility Stakes. This is an individual competition over a full agility course. In 1989 and 1990 there were 16 heats with the 1st and 2nd winners qualifying directly for the final held at Olympia in December.

This year 1991, the qualification has reverted back to the earlier system with the top 10 dogs from each of 12 heats qualifying for semi-finals held at the East of England Show and Stoneleigh Town and Country Show. The best 5 dogs from each of the 6 semi-finals will go through to the Final at Olympia.

Dave Powell & Kenour Katie,
winner 1988 & '89.

Some top mini dogs and handlers at Pedigree's Olympia Final.

The Pedigree Chum Mini Agility Stakes. This is for dogs under 15" (381mm) at the shoulder and also has its final at Olympia.

The Pedigree Chum Inter Club Team Stakes. A team competition for four dogs and handlers with prizes in the final of over £1,000 worth of kit or equipment for the six winning clubs.

The Pedigree Chum Gamblers Stakes. A gamblers competition with 12 heats. The 1st and 2nd winners qualifying for the final which is held at the City of Birmingham Championship Dog Show in September.

The Pedigree Chum Two-Dog Relay. Teams of two handlers and dogs compete over the same course which has no contact equipment in it. When the first dog finishes the course there is a baton change between the handlers. The dogs' combined score and time gives the result with the 1st and 2nd winners qualifying for the final, again held at the City of Birmingham Championship Dog Show.

Also at this show is the Kennel Club Junior Organisation's Agility Final, open to the youngsters with a competition for the under 12's and another for the over 12's. This is very popular and there are some excellent juniors competing.

Another big competition for two handlers and dogs is The Barbour Knockout Pairs Challenge. Eight nationwide heats are held producing 64 pairs who compete on a knockout basis at the final which is held at the Royal Show in July.

Also sponsored by Barbour is the Barbour Clockwatcher for senior dogs only, also with the final at the Royal Show.

An individual knockout competition is sponsored by Spillers each year, called the Spillers Shapes Knockout Tournament. Eight heats are held with eight dogs qualifying from each heat for the final. This is held at the Middlesex Show where the 64 dogs compete in a very exciting competition. Dogs seem to love this sort of knockout and get very excited which makes a thrilling final.

Also at the Middlesex Show is the final of the Winalot Prime Starters Agility Dog of the Year Competition. This is for beginners to the sport who have not won a first prize.

Tex Chunks and Royal Canin also sponsor Agility Classes with Grand Finals held at big shows.

Everyone dreams of competing at Crufts and many clubs work really hard all year training for the Crufts Inter Club Competition. This is another team competition with four dogs and handlers. There are eight national heats each producing one winning club which qualifies for the final held in the big ring at Crufts.

Crufts winning team 1989 & 1990. South Humberside D. T. C.

Notes

3
MINI AGILITY

Small dogs, those not exceeding 15" at the shoulder compete in the mini classes. These are getting more and more popular and a lot of shows now include mini classes in their schedule. The big qualifier for minis is the Pedigree Chum Mini Agility Stakes which has its final at Olympia in December. Eukanuba sponsor a mini agility tournament with the final at Crufts.

The Agility Club recommendations for mini agility state the following:
"That all equipment used for Mini Classes should be to the standard sizes used for larger dogs with the exception of a table which should be a maximum of 15" high. For preference a pause box should replace the table.
Hurdles: Height maximum 15".
Tyre: Height to centre of aperture maximum 20".
Long Jump: Length 3' maximum. The height of the boards in relation to the dogs competing should be taken into consideration by the Judge.
Weaving Poles: Maximum distance apart 2'.

What special problems do minis have and should some of the standard equipment be adapted for minis?

'A' Frame: Although most mini dogs will try very hard to get over this obstacle, some 'A' Frames with slats further apart than 12" really present them with a formidable task. This obstacle can be particularly difficult for the very small dog such as a Yorkshire Terrier.

To be fair for all sizes of mini the slats on an 'A' frame need to be at least every 12" starting 1' from the bottom, not 2' as so many do now.

Bigger dogs rarely use this bottom 2' but minis have to and need the extra slat. Often they need an extra one at the top as well. It may be amusing to see a little dog scrabbling about trying to get a grip, but it isn't fair to the dog

See-Saw: Some see-saws are very heavy and a mini dog may be almost at the end of the board before his weight is sufficient to tip it. It may then bang down very quickly, which can be very off-putting for the dog. A see-saw made to tip when a very light dog just passes the centre is surely fairer and much safer for all.

The surface on the see-saw and also on the dog walk needs to be really rough to help these small dogs.

Long jump: At most shows the first three or four boards of an ordinary sized long jump are used for minis. This is all right so long as they are not too wide or too high.

Some long jump boards are so high that using them for minis means giving the dog a 3' spread at near his maximum height (15"). It isn't surprising that the long jump is the obstacle that causes most problems for minis.

I think a mini long jump should be a separate piece of equipment, a scaled down version of the big long jump with at least five boards, each narrower than normal. The height of the boards should not exceed 7" and as the minimum length of 3' is very hard for the small mini, I feel 2'6" maximum would be fairer.

Collapsible tunnel: The normal collapsible tunnel can be very heavy for the mini dog and when wet can be almost impossible. A shorter tunnel made of light weight material would be much more inviting.

Tyre: Some suspended tyres present an extra problem. When lowered to mini height, the bottom chains become almost horizontal at approximately 15" high (mini height), so inviting the dogs to jump them instead of going through the tyre.

Weaving poles: Very few minis really bend as they weave, most taking several strides between each of the poles. I wonder if having the poles closer, say 15" apart, would make this a more interesting obstacle for this group. Also, perhaps 8 to 10 poles should be the maximum number.

Course design for a mini dog round needs careful thought. Jumps placed far apart will make loss of interest a real problem for some. To test real control between jumps, perhaps some should be placed closer than the Kennel Club minimum of 4 yards. It seems logical that jumps could safely be closer for minis.

One of the biggest problems with mini classes at the moment is that the one class has to cater for minis of all sizes. The very tiny 8" or 9" dog has to compete alongside the 14" or 15" dog. Is this really fair?

Maybe another class is needed, perhaps dividing the minis into dogs under 12" and dogs between 12" and 15". As the numbers of minis competing increases this may well be possible and would surely be fairer for the very small mini.

All these are merely my ideas on mini agility, but I do feel more thought is needed from all concerned.

A mini dog weaving

4
YOUR FIRST SHOW

It is always as well to give yourself plenty of time when arriving at your first show. You are bound to be feeling very nervous and tense and having to rush won't help.

Arriving with at least three quarters of an hour before briefing time will mean you can exercise your dogs, find the toilets, collect your numbers, take stock of the situation and maybe even have a quick cup of coffee, all without panicking.

There will usually be 2 or 3 rings, so next you want to find out which classes are on first and see which courses you will need to walk.

After you have walked the course, probably hardly taking it in as this is your first show, it will be time for the judge's briefing.

The beginner to agility shows may find this briefing too brief, with the judge saying *"Standard rules apply, 5 faults for everything."* What, the beginner may ask, are Standard Rules?

Standard Rules just means Standard Marking of faults as laid down in the K.C. Rules for agility:

MARKING.
A. Standard marking.
All courses faults in units of five. For time faults see paragraph b below.

1. Table-Pause - faulted at judge's discretion.
2. See-Saw - must be touching the ground before the dog alights from the obstacle.
3. Wishing Well - a dog should be faulted if it touches the base or dislodges the pole.
4. Long Jump and Water Jump - a dog should be faulted if it touches any part of the obstacle.
5. Hurdle/Wall - a dog should not be faulted if any part of the obstacle is touched and does not fall.
6. Weaving poles - (Maximum 2 faults) incorrect entry - one fault (not to be classed as a refusal) - further error one fault - failure to complete correctly before continuing to the next obstacle elimination.
7. All other obstacles - fault for failure to negotiate correctly.
8. Refusal/Runout - fault for each refusal/runout.
9. Three refusals/runouts - elimination.
10. Out of control - elimination.
11. Taking the wrong course - elimination.
12. Contact area - fault for each failure to make contact.
13. Course time - at the judges discretion.

B. Cumulative Marking/Time Faults.
Faults incurred for failure to negotiate obstacle will be added to the faults incurred for failure to complete course in set time. A single fault will be added for each second, or part thereof over the set time.

C. Other Marking.
Any variation in the form of marking must be clearly defined to all competitors prior to competition.

Even reading this, however, the beginner will still have many questions and to help answer these I am going to go through the various pieces of equipment and explain the points to watch.

THE START

This is usually marked by two poles which most judges see as markers for the time-keeper and not as an obstacle. The clock starts when the dog passes in between these poles.

Occasionally electronic timing is used and the clock starts when the timing beam is broken, so if you wish to leave your dog at the start and get ahead on the course, you must be careful to walk round the timing device and not through the beam. The dog

Some start lines are marked with poles, or at top competitions, electronic timers. Shown here a dog crosses the start line triggering the timer. She is also clocked by a human timekeeper as a safety check. Note the same configuration at the finish line.

must be the one to break the beam. This can cause problems with a dog who is not too steady at the start and who may run to the handler.

With ordinary poles to mark the start it doesn't usually matter whether the handler walks through the poles, although many handlers do go round, so training themselves for electronic timing.

Occasionally a judge will decide to treat the start as an electronic one and want the handlers to walk round the poles. In this case this would be covered in the judge's briefing.

At one time, starting from the table was common, now it is rarely used except in Gamblers. If it is used, the clock starts as the dog leaves the table. The judge will say in his briefing if he requires the dog down on the table at the start, otherwise any position will do.

THE FINISH

Again this is normally marked by two poles, which also most judges take as markers for the time-keeper and not an obstacle to be negotiated by the dog. The time-keeper stops the clock as the dog passes the poles.

A few judges, however, still persist in making the finish an extra obstacle by placing the poles too distant from the last obstacle and by saying that the dog must pass in between the poles before the clock is stopped. In this case if the dog runs past on the wrong side of the pole (outside it) the handler must be prepared to call the dog back and make him go through inside the poles before the clock is stopped. This arrangement is, in my opinion, bad judging, but the beginner should be prepared.

A bad finish

A good finish.

A GOOD FINISH   A POOR FINISH

A good finish has the poles close enough to the last obstacle and wide enough apart so the dog easily runs through.

OBSTACLE MARKING.

Hurdles

A knockdown of any pole or part of a jump costs 5 faults. Refusing or running past a jump also costs 5 faults. Jumping the wing instead of the centre of the jump is counted as a refusal and the jump must be done again correctly or elimination will result.

A dog jumping the wing.

A refusal is when the dog stops dead in front of any obstacle and refuses to do it, having to be brought back to try again.

Also in agility, a refusal is given when the dog runs past the line of the jump (or indeed any piece of equipment), the dog can therefore be penalised without even attempting the obstacle.

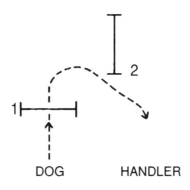

In the example the handler was too far behind or too slow with commands. The dog, therefore, ran past jump 2 to the handler, thus getting a refusal for passing the line of jump 2.

If, after running past a jump, the dog comes back under the jump, this is a wrong course and results in elimination.

In show jumping, a horse gets a refusal if it turns its back on a jump and a few judges will apply this to dogs, so a dog circling before a jump could be given a refusal.

If a jump is down when you get to it, either because the wind blew it down or someone forgot to rebuild it after the preceding dog, you must make your dog jump any poles still up or run between the wings if the whole jump is down; not doing so could be counted as a wrong course.

If the poles have blown down the dog must still go between the wings.

The wall

This has removable bricks on the top. If the dog knocks a brick which moves but does not fall, he will be lucky and not be faulted.

Wall with brick displaced but still there.

The well

This is different and the dog will get 5 faults if he stands on the body of the well even if he doesn't knock the pole off.

Dog standing on the well.

Long jump

The dog will be faulted if it touches any part of the long jump.

The long jump has 4 corner poles to stop the dog cross jumping. The marking of this may differ. I judge a dog which goes through the front 2 poles but out at the side as not doing the obstacle correctly so give him 5 faults, but the dog doesn't do the obstacle again. See example.

The long jump has four corner poles.

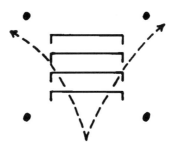

E.g. 1

DOG GOES EITHER WAY

However, a dog which doesn't pass between the front poles is not starting the obstacle correctly, so I give him 5 faults for a refusal and he must do the obstacle again.

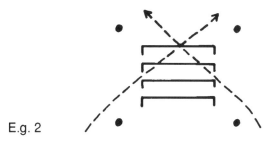

E.g. 2

Other judges may call example 1 a refusal, so it's as well to find out how the long jump is being judged.

Water jump
This has 4 corner poles which are usually marked the same as for the long jump, the dog also getting 5 faults for putting a foot in the water.

The water jump also has corner poles.

Tyre

If the tyre is well staked a knock down is impossible, so refusals and run pasts are the only faults here. With the type of tyre that is suspended on chains a dog may get a refusal for running under the tyre or jumping through at the side. A dog coming back under or through at the side will be eliminated for a wrong course.

Dogs are not faulted for standing on the tyre as they jump through.

The dog runs under the tyre, this is a refusal.

Table

This is at the judge's discretion but normally a dog which runs past or goes under the table will get 5 faults for a refusal.

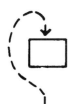

In starter classes most judges will not fault a dog that runs round the table and jumps on from the back, but in higher classes this would count as a refusal.

Occasionally a judge will only allow the dog to get on from the front, giving a refusal for passing the start of the table to jump on from the side, but normally the dog is allowed 3 sides to get on.

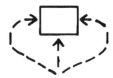

A refusal with the dog going under the table.

A dog that jumps on and straight off again will be given 5 faults even if he slides off. During the 5 second count the dog must stay in the 'down' position and the count will stop if he gets up and will not resume until he is lying down again. Normally this is not faulted but is a waste of time.

A dog that anticipates the 'go' and doesn't get back on the table can be given 5 faults or be eliminated at the judge's discretion.

Tunnels

Refusals and run pasts cost 5 faults.

A dog who puts any part of himself, even if its just his nose, into a tunnel that is not the required course, will be eliminated.

'A' frame and dog walk

Failure to make contact with the coloured area, either going up or down, will gain the dog 5 faults. Jumping off at the side is also 5 faults. Where the dog jumps off is important; if the dog jumps off before passing the apex of the 'A' frame or before beginning the down plank of the dog walk, it counts as a refusal and the dog must do the obstacle again. Failure to do so would result in elimination.

A dog, however, that jumps off after these points gets 5 faults, but should continue and not do the obstacle again.

The dog jumps over the contact area and so gets 5 faults.

The see-saw must be touching the ground before the dog gets off.

See saw

Contacts are marked as for the 'A' frame and dog walk. Dogs that jump off before the centre point are given a refusal, but the dog must also stay on the obstacle until it touches the ground. A dog who flies off is risking injury and so gets 5 faults even if he does touch the contact.

With all the contact equipment, run pasts are counted as refusals and given 5 faults.

Weaving poles

Normally in starter classes the dog gets 5 faults for an incorrect entry.

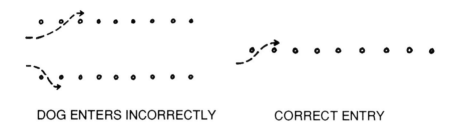

DOG ENTERS INCORRECTLY   CORRECT ENTRY

Any further faults in the poles are not usually faulted so long as they are corrected.

In classes other than starters, 5 faults are charged for incorrect entry, then another 5 faults for any other mistakes, making a maximum of 10 faults possible in the poles.

In all classes the poles must be completed correctly before going onto the next obstacle, or the dog is eliminated.

Touching your dog is not allowed and every time you knee the dog in the weaving poles it will cost you 5 faults.

As well as faults incurred at obstacles, the handler should also be aware of the following points.

Deliberately touching any equipment or the dog costs the handler 5 faults.

Three refusals at any time on the course, not necessarily at one obstacle, result in elimination.

The dog running out of the ring, out of control, is eliminated. If the ropes of the ring are very close and the dog is obviously under control, simply jumping big and overshooting out of the ring, he will not normally be faulted.

The dog fouling the ring, wearing a collar in the ring, or the handler carrying food or anything in his hands, also results in elimination.

Taking the wrong course at any time also gets the big 'E'. This includes jumping back over any obstacle just done and putting a foot back on a contact obstacle. The exception to this is when a judge sets a course that requires the dog to go straight back over an obstacle just completed.

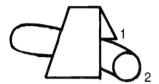

THE DOG DOES 1. THEN IN
TURNING FOR 2, STEPS BACK
ONTO 1. RESULT: ELIMINATION.

I hope that after reading all these ways to get eliminated the beginner will not be put off having a go. We were all beginners once and everyone in agility is very friendly. If you tell the ring caller and the judge that this is your first show, I'm sure most will help you if you get into difficulties.

5

WALKING THE COURSE

Before any agility competition handlers are given the opportunity to walk the course. This gives the handler the chance to decide how he hopes to handle his dog on the various sections of the course.

I like to walk a course two or three times. The first time I just try to get the whole course in my mind so, hopefully, I know where to go. I then walk it again deciding how I will handle my dog, dividing the course into sections in my mind and sorting out what I hope will be best. Finally I walk it a third time as I plan to work it.

It can be difficult to decide exactly what is best with a hundred or so other people also walking the course. So afterwards I like to view the course while the first few dogs are working and really get in my mind, my plan of action.

With a really fast dog, knowing what you hope to do is essential and walking the course is very important.

A beginner handler may find it hard to keep the course in mind as he is worrying too much about what the dog will do. Walking the course with an experienced handler and discussing the various sections can be a big help.

Let's look at a typical course and see the various points you need to think about.

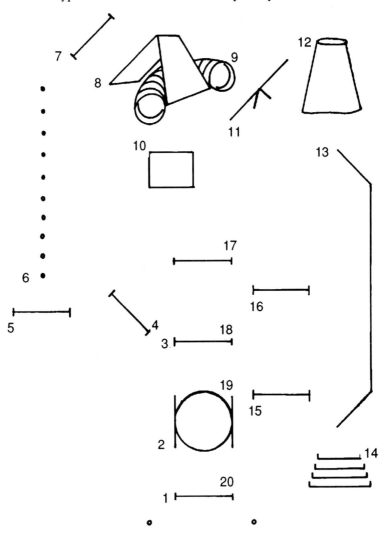

Right from the start decisions have to be made.

How far back from the start do you leave the dog? Not on the line: you want him to have speed up before the clock starts, but if you leave him too far back is he likely to knock the first fence down?

Do you make him wait at the start and get ahead on the course? Or do you run with him? If so, do you run on his right or left? If you make him wait, how far should you go and where should you stand when you call him?

The answers all depend on your dog. What you would do with one dog wouldn't necessarily be the right thing with a different dog.

First, whether to leave the dog at the start. This can be an advantage as the handler can get a head start on the dog and may then be in a better position to prevent him going on over number 17 after jump number 3.

However, there can be problems in leaving the dog. Firstly is he likely to creep, maybe even past the start pole? Is he more likely to flatten over jump 1 and knock it down because he is in such a hurry to join you? Is he at all likely to run round a jump? Number 2 is a tyre which many dogs will run past. If you are calling the dog down a row of obstacles which include a tyre, it is always best to keep eye contact through the hole in the tyre. The dog, then, is less likely to run past it. All these points must be considered if you leave your dog at the start.

If you run with the dog or leave him and only go as far as number 2, on which side do you run? Jump number 17 is probably more inviting to the dog than number 4. Do you run with your dog on your left and hope to block number 17 with your body? Or do you run with your dog on the right and give him a sharp command to turn him left after number 3?

I find the majority of dogs, providing they are used to working either side of the handler, keep their attention on the handler. So handling the dog on the right down jumps 1 to 3, the handler should have little difficulty turning the dog for number 4.

If you decide to handle the dog on the right for this section you must next decide where to change the dog over to your left ready for the weaving poles and the right hand loop to the 'A' frame. I find it safest for the handler to change sides behind the dog as a general rule, so the best place would be behind jump 5, sending the dog over first and running round to the right of the jump.

Changing sides when necessary, behind and not in front of the dog, is best for several reasons.

1. You don't need to take your eyes off the dog if behind him. Even a split second or two, when you can't see what the dog is doing, can produce some nasty surprises.

2. If you run across in front of the dog, you break his line of vision to the next obstacle and a knock down is more likely.

3. There is always the risk of a collision with the dog if the handler runs across in front, particularly if the dog is coming out of the tunnel.

Now back to the course. While walking this section containing the weaving poles, remember to work out which way your dog should leave the poles. Then you will be sure he has done them correctly.

It's straight forward now until number 9, the tunnel under the 'A' frame. You must decide how best to negotiate the tunnel, whilst trying to keep your dog on the 'A' frame contact. Will you step over the tunnel or go round it? You also need to plan the best way of preventing your dog stepping back onto the 'A' frame as you turn him to the tunnel.

Right, onto the table. Where do you go next? A lot of time can be saved by turning the dog to face the direction he will leave the table, before you 'down' him. Obviously this is not possible if the dog is a long way ahead of you as you approach the table, but if you are up with your dog it is well worth trying.

If you want to walk over to the next obstacle while the dog is in the 'down', he will be a lot less likely to move if facing you.

After number 11 how far do you need to run up to the tunnel? Can you send your dog? This tunnel has an awkward angle of entry and it may be safer, particularly with a beginner dog, to go right up to the entrance with the dog.

Numbers 13 and 14 look fairly straight forward, only watch the long jump. Many dogs, including my Heidi, don't think a long jump is much of an obstacle and they may prefer number 15.

The long jump negotiated, do you need to run past it or can you turn the dog right and call him back to number 15? It will save your legs if you can.

Number 16 now. Are you going to run all the way round to come back down the home straight with your dog on your left? Or do you change sides again? If so, where to change? Before or after number 16?

Again, it depends on your dog, but you need to ensure the dog won't cut in too sharply after number 16 and get a refusal for passing the line of number 17. It may be better to change sides at number 17.

Watch the angle at which you put the dog over number 17 or he may land heading for number 4.

Hopefully numbers 18 - 20 should prove quite straight forward.

Even when you have walked the course carefully and planned your strategy, you still need to be ready to change your plans in a split second if your dog does something unpredictable. I find that when things go wrong it is usually something totally unexpected that catches you out, not the obvious traps.

Gamblers Courses

Before you can start to plan your course in a Gamblers Class you need to know the following:

1. The amount of time allowed on the course.
2. Whether you can do an obstacle twice consecutively, e.g. back jump hurdles.
3. Whether you are able to do value 2 and 3 obstacles consecutively, or if you have to do a value 1 obstacle in between.
4. Can you jump the long jump both ways?
5. What the joker is and how long you have to do it.
6. Any other points the judge is looking for e.g. occasionally the four corner obstacles gain extra points if all four are done.

Once you have all these facts, given in the judge's briefing, you can start to plan your course.

Although back jumping and going straight back over a contact, or doing the poles twice consecutively (if allowed) can save time, with a beginner dog it is often better to choose a little course and maybe go round it twice than to keep stopping the dog. Again it all depends on your dog.

Ideally you want to finish your given time in the close vicinity of the joker; you may need a lot of practice in Gambler classes before you can judge this really well. So, when the whistle goes for the joker, don't panic, just calmly take your dog there and have a go. You may be surprised at what you can do.

A typical joker

Pairs Courses

Here you and your partner need to decide which of the two dogs should run first. In classes where both pairs run separately this does not matter, but in classes with a baton change in the middle, the first handler has to get back as well as the dog before the second partner can start, while at the end it is the second dog that stops the clock whether the second handler is up with him at the finish or not.

So in this type of class it makes sense to run the fastest dog last, if the handler cannot keep up with the dog.

Learning from your mistakes

If things go wrong and your dog does something unexpected, take a few moments afterwards to stand and think how you could have handled the situation differently. We all make mistakes, but if you can learn from them you will be better prepared next time.

I also find it interesting and valuable to watch other handlers with similar dogs to mine, to see how they tackle the various courses.

6

WARM UP EXERCISES

I always believe you should warm up your dog before competing or obstacle training. As well as physically loosening the muscles, this warm up session helps to get the dog mentally in tune with the handler.

You don't need to take the dog over a jump to warm him up for agility. I find fast heel-work is much better. I find it loosens me up too.

In a training course, it is during this warm up heel-work that I begin to teach the beginner dog the right and left turns which are so essential later on.

Although it is quite possible to do this simply by running in and out of the obstacles on the course, I find beginners are better with definite aims, so I set them warm up exercises. Here are a few examples:

Exercise 1

Equipment: 2 parallel lines of poles about 6 paces apart. 10 to 12 poles in all. The poles in line 2 are spaced in between those of line 1.

The handler and dog zig-zag between the two lines, the handler giving the appropriate left and right commands.

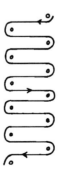

This exercise can be varied in the following ways:

1. The handler can alter the speed, keeping the dog's attention all the time.

2. The dog can be 'downed' and made to wait while the handler carries on then either returns to the dog, or calls him to heel.

Exercise 2

Equipment: 3 hurdles approximately 8 paces apart. 4 poles - 2 at each side about 4 paces out from the line of jumps.

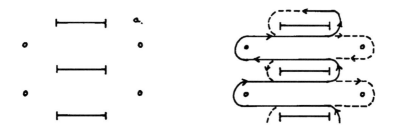

The handler runs with the dog at his side turning sharp right at each pole and left round each jump. At the last jump the handler continues right round and then comes back using the poles on the other side.

This exercise is also good training for passing close to jumps without the dog doing them.

Exercise 3

Equipment: 2 hurdles and a pipe tunnel about 6 paces apart. 4 poles - 2 at each side about 4 paces from the line of jumps.

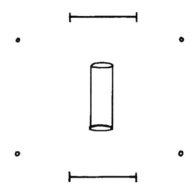

The handler turns sharp round the jump and first pole, allows the dog to go through the tunnel, then carries on round the next pole and jump, coming back on the other side and through the tunnel again.

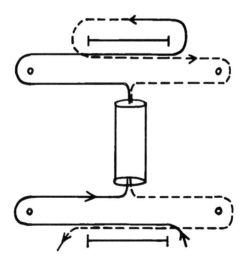

This exercise is also good for teaching control as the dog leaves the tunnel.

Exercise 4

For 2 or more dogs.

Equipment: 4 hurdles about 6 paces apart. Table.

The first handler and dog starts by the table, zig-zags in and out of the jumps, goes right round the last jump and zig-zags back to finish at the table. This dog is then put onto the table and he stays in the 'down' when the second handler and dog zig-zags round the jumps. The first dog is called off the table in time for the second dog to finish there.

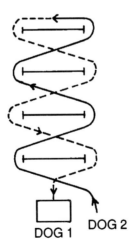

DOG 1   DOG 2

All these exercises can be done on the lead with beginner dogs. However, as with all training in agility, the aim should be to lose the lead as soon as possible. Occasionally I also do these exercises with the dog on the handler's right.

7
JUMPING EXERCISES

As with the jumping exercises in '*Agility is Fun*' (Book 1), the following exercises can be used both with beginner and experienced dogs. They can be done with low height jumps if the dogs are not ready for full height.

It is not necessarily intended for all the stages of any one exercise to be done at the same training session. How much you cover depends on your dog. Some dogs can do a lot of training happily, while others get bored quickly. Never try to do too much and always keep it fun, giving lots of praise and play (p & p).

Exercise 1.

Aim of exercise: to teach the dog to pay attention; practise of send away to the table; directional control.

Equipment: row of three jumps and the table. At least 5 paces between the obstacles. Also 2 jumps placed at the sides.

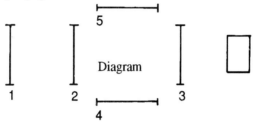

Teaching the dog to do an agility send away to the table is fully covered in the first book, jumping exercise 4.

1. Starting in front of jump 1 the handler sends the dog over jumps 1, 2 and 3 to the table. 'Down' the dog on the table for a few seconds before praising.

2. Send the dog over jumps 1 and 2, then command him to turn right and send him over jump 4. (P & p).

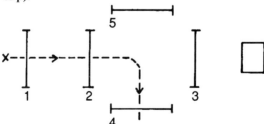

3. Send the dog over jumps 1 and 2 then command him to turn left and send him over jump 5. (P & p).

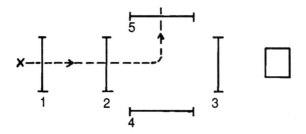

At first the handler will need to run with the dog, but you should work towards being able to stay further and further back until you can do stages 1 - 3 from behind jump 1.

4. Repeat stage 1. Leaving the dog in the 'down' on the table, the handler goes to stand in front of jump 3. Recall the dog over jump 3. Command the dog to turn left and send him over jump 4. (Remember when the dog is jumping towards you and you turn him to your right, he actually turns left). (P & p).

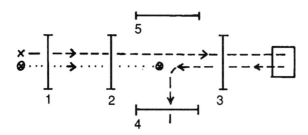

5. Repeat stage 1. While the dog is 'down' on the table the handler goes to stand in front of jump 3. Recall the dog over jump 3, then command him to turn right and send him over jump 5. (P & p).

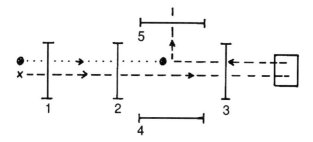

6. Starting in front of jump 1, send the dog over jumps 1, 2 and 3 and onto the table. 'Down' for at least 5 seconds, then recall over jumps 3, 2 and 1. The handler remains in front of jump 1. (P & p).

With all these stages, when the dog 'downs' on the table, it is important to make him 'stay' for at least 5 seconds. Never let the dog jump straight back off.

Exercise 2.

Aim of exercise: to teach the dog to do bounce jumps i.e. land from one jump and take off again immediately.

Equipment: three hurdles - practise on hurdles with wings and also hurdles without wings. When first doing this exercise have at least 5 paces (4 yards) between the centres of the jumps. Decrease this until the dog can do it with only 4 paces (3 yards) between.

First set up the jumps for a right turn.

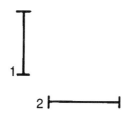

43

1. Leave the dog at X and stand behind jump 1. Call the dog over jump 1. Command him to turn right and send him over jump 2. (P & p)

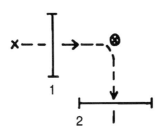

2. Leave the dog at X and stand between the two jumps as shown. Call the dog over jump 1 and send on over jump 2. (P & p)

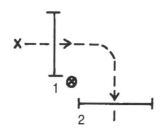

3. With the dog on the handler's left, send him over jump 1. Command him to turn right and send him over jump 2. The handler moves over as shown. (P & p).

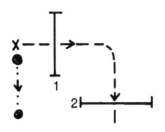

Now set up the jumps for a left turn.

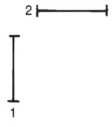

4. Leave the dog at X and stand behind jump 1. Call the dog over jump 1. Command him to turn left and send him over jump 2. (P & p).

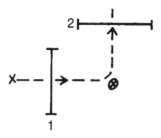

5. Leave the dog at X and stand between the two jumps as shown. Call the dog over jump 1 and send him on over jump 2. (P & p).

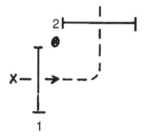

6. With the dog on the handler's right, send him over jump 1. Command him to turn left and send him over jump 2. The handler moves over as shown. (p & p)

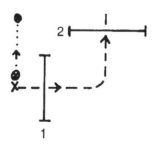

Some dogs can do this type of jump quite easily. Others may need to be told to 'wait' or 'steady'.

At first use jumps with several poles on them. Later remove the lower poles until he can do it on single pole jumps. When this exercise is used in competition, the second jump is usually a single pole and many dogs run under it.

7. Combine the two turns.

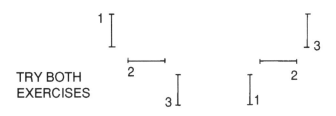

TRY BOTH
EXERCISES

Experiment to discover which side you find the easiest to work your dog.

Exercise 3.

Aim of exercise: directional control and paying attention to the handler.

Equipment: Square of jumps 5 - 8 paces apart, depending on experience of dog.

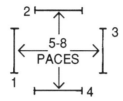

1. Starting in the centre of the square, send the dog over jump 1. Command him to turn right and bring him back into the square over jump 2. (P & p).

The handler may need to move as shown to help the dog.

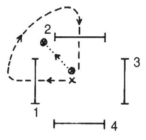

2. Send the dog over jump 1. Command him to turn left and bring him back into the square over jump 4. (P & p).

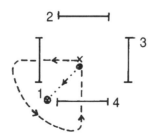

3. Send the dog over jump 1. Command him to turn right, then call him back into the square in between jumps 1 and 2. (P & p)

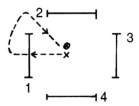

4. Send the dog over jump 1. Command him to turn left, then call him back into the square in between jumps 1 and 4. (P & p)

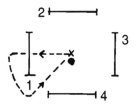

5. Send the dog out over jumps 1, 2, 3 and 4 in turn, working in a clockwise direction and calling the dog back into the square in between the jumps each time. (P & p).

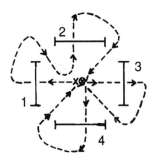

As the dog comes back into the square the handler should give him a command to turn left, trying to turn the dog in front of himself each time. Try to avoid the dog going round the back of the handler to heel each time, this is a waste of time.

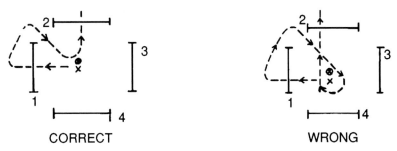

CORRECT   WRONG

6. Repeat stage 5, but working in an anti-clockwise direction. The dog now turns left after each jump and right in front of the handler in the square before the next jump. (P & p).

7. Send the dog over jump 1. Command him to turn right, then bring him back into the square over jump 2. Command him to turn left, then send him over jump 3 and back in over jump 4. (P & p). The handler may need to move to the edge of the square to ensure the dog goes far enough out.

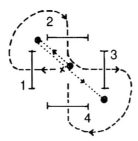

8. Repeat 7, working in the opposite direction.

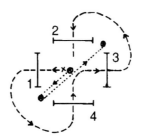

Exercise 4.

Aim of exercise: directional control.

Equipment: Square of jumps as in Exercise 3.

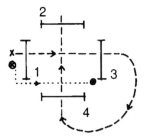

1. Working with the dog on the handler's left, send the dog over jump 1, then jump 3. Command him to turn right and send him over jump 4, then jump 2. (P & p).

2. Working with the dog on the handler's right, send him over jumps 1 and 3. Command him to turn left and then send him over jumps 2 and 4. (P & p).

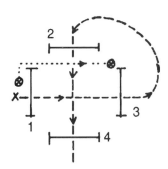

3. Working with the dog on the left, send him over jumps 1 and 3, then command him to turn right and send him over jump 4, then left and over jump 1. (P & p)

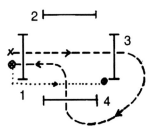

4. With the dog on the right, send him over jumps 1 and 3. Command him to turn left and send him over jump 2. Then turn right and send him over jump 1. (P & p)

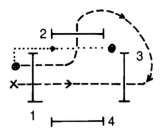

Exercise 5.

Aim of exercise: more directional control.

Equipment: Square of jumps as used in Exercises 3 and 4.

For the whole of this exercise the handler should try to stay outside the square of jumps.

1. Send the dog over jump 1, then jump 3. (P & p).

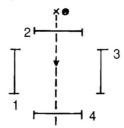

2. Send the dog over jump 2, then jump 4. (P & p).

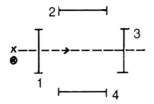

3. Send the dog over jump 1. Command him to turn right and send him on over jump 4. (P & p). Try to stay outside the square simply moving over as shown if necessary.

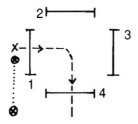

4. Send the dog over jump 1. Command him to turn left and send him on over jump 2. (P & p).

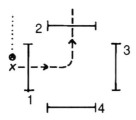

5. Send the dog over jump 1. Command him to turn right and send him over jump 4, then turn the dog left and send him over jump 3. Now turn him right again and send him over jump 2. (P & p).

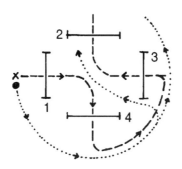

The handler moves on the outside of the square as shown.

How wide the handler and dog will need to go between jumps 4 and 3 will depend on the experience of the dog. Some dogs can jump from really close to the jump, others will need more run. Always be fair to the dog, don't ask the impossible.

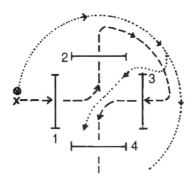

6. Repeat 5 working in the opposite direction. (P & p).

This is an exercise for the handler to practise working outside the square. In competition however you may find it better to do 5 or 6 moving in for the last jump as shown in the diagrams. Try both ways.

Exercise 6.
Aim of exercise: back jumping on command.
Equipment: square of jumps as in Exercise 3.

1. Handler stays in the centre of the square. Send dog over jump 1, then call him back over jump 1. Command the dog to turn to his left and send him over jump 2, then call him back over jump 2. (P & p).

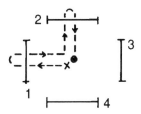

If you wish, you can then continue in a clockwise direction repeating this with jumps 3 and 4.

2. Repeat stage 1 working anti-clockwise.

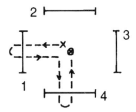

You must be sure the dog only back-jumps on command; this is not an exercise I would do too often or with a beginner dog.

3. The handler stays outside the square. Send the dog over jump 1. Command him to turn right and send him over jump 4, then send him back over jump 4. (P & p).

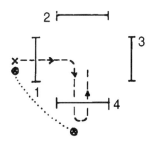

This time the dog is jumping away from the handler on the repeated jump. If you wish you can continue over jumps 3 and 2.

4. Repeat stage 3 in a clockwise direction.

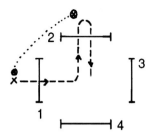

Exercise 7.

Aim of exercise: practise of jumps in a straight line, but off set.
Equipment: 4 hurdles set up as below.

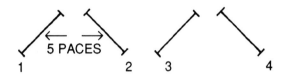

1. Handler runs with the dog doing jumps 1 - 4 in order. (P & p).
Try this, handling the dog both sides and find which suits you best.

2. Leaving the dog behind jump 1, the handler stands in between jumps 2 and 3. Call the dog over jumps 1 and 2 and then send him on over jumps 3 and 4. (P & p).

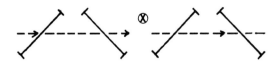

3. Repeat stage 1, but the handler should try to hang back further and further directing the dog by voice alone. (P & p).

Repeat stages 1 to 3, doing the jumps in reverse order.

Exercise 8.

Aim of exercise: speeding up the slow dog.

Equipment: 4 hurdles set up as below.

The handler stays in the centre for both these, leaving the dog in front of jump 1.

1. Send the dog round the jumps in order in a clockwise direction. (P & p).

2. Send the dog round the jumps in reverse order in an anti-clockwise direction. (P & p)

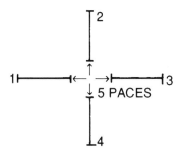

Some dogs really enjoy this exercise and it can speed them up considerably.

You can vary it by changing direction with a back jump, and also by finishing at a different jump each time and calling the dog into you for praise.

Exercise 9.

Aim of exercise: directional control and paying attention to handler.
Equipment: 2 squares of jumps 6 paces apart.

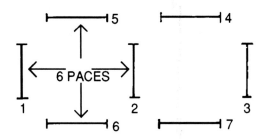

This is a continuation of Exercise 7 in 'Agility is Fun', book 1. That exercise should be worked through before trying the following.

1. With the dog on the handler's left, send him over jumps 1 and 2. Command him to turn right. Send the dog over jump 7, turn him right over jump 6, then right again over jump 2 and finally straight on over jump 3. (P & p).

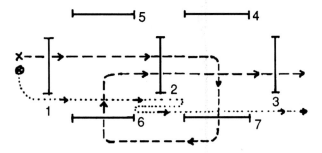

2. With the dog on the handler's right, send him over jumps 1 and 2. Command him to turn left and send him over jump 4; then turn the dog left again over jump 5, then jump 2, before sending him straight on over jump 3. (P & p).

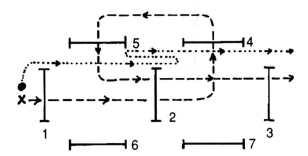

3. Working the dog on the left and giving him the appropriate directional commands send him over jumps 1 and 2, then jumps 7 and 6, and finally jump 1 again. (P & p).

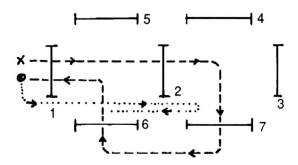

4. Work the dog on the right. Send him over jumps 1 and 2, then jumps 4 and 5, and finally jump 1 again. (P & p).

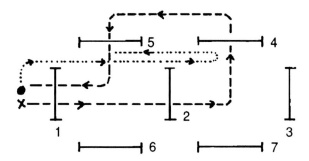

Notes

OBSTACLE TRAINING

Once the dog has been taught to do the various agility obstacles (see 'Agility is Fun', Book 1) he needs lots of practice.

The following exercises are designed to allow the handler to practise each obstacle several times without boring the dog.

I have grouped the exercises for each obstacle together, but normally only one, or part of one, would be done at a training session.

TRAINING EXERCISES, USING CONTACT EQUIPMENT

'A' frame

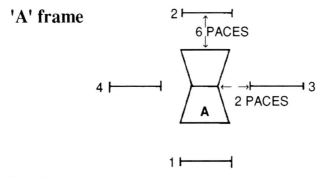

Exercise 1.

Aim of exercise: practising turning in different directions after the obstacle.

Equipment: 'A' frame and 4 hurdles.

1. Working with the dog on the left. Send dog over jump 1, do 'A', then jump 2. Command the dog to turn right and send him over jump 3. (P & p).

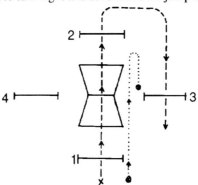

Equipment set up for Exercise 1.

2. Working with the dog on the right, send the dog over jump 1, do 'A', then jump 2. Command the dog to turn left and send him over jump 4. (P & p).

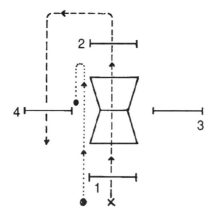

3. With the dog on the handler's left, send him over jump 1, do 'A', then turn him right and send him over jump 3. (p & p)

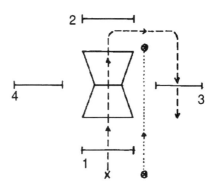

4. With the dog on the handler's right, send him over jump 1, do 'A' then turn him left over jump 4. (p & p)

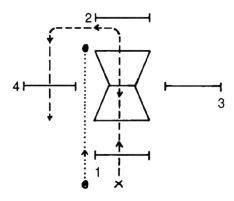

With practice you should be able to leave the dog at X and stand half-way along the 'A' frame for each of stages 1 - 4, just moving enough to ensure the dog gets both contacts.

Exercise 2.
Aim of Exercise: getting onto the 'A' frame from different angles.
Equipment: 'A' frame and 4 hurdles.

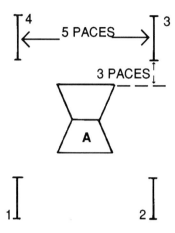

As the dog gets proficient at this exercise, the jumps may be moved nearer to the 'A' frame.

1. With the dog on the handler's left, do 'A', turn right, and send dog over jumps 3 and 2, then do 'A' again. (P & p).

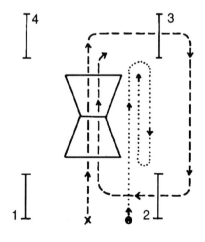

2. With the dog on the handler's right, do 'A', turn left and do jumps 4 and 1, then do 'A' again. (P & p).

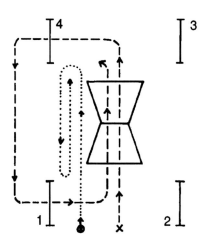

3. Leave the dog at X and stand on the right of 'A'. Call the dog over jump 1. Do 'A', turn the dog right and send him over jump 3. (P & p). The handler moves as shown.

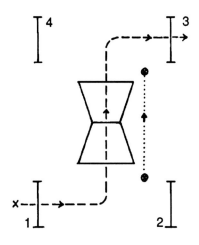

4. Leave the dog at Y and stand on the left of 'A'. Call the dog over jump 2. Do 'A', turn the dog left and send him over jump 4. (P & p).

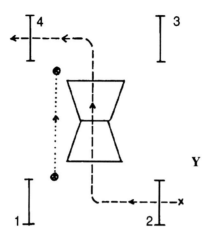

At first, when approaching the 'A' frame from an angle, the handler must ensure the dog is straight before he starts up the 'A' frame. As the dog gets more experienced he will learn to straighten himself.

Exercise 3.

Aim of Exercise: practising getting onto the 'A' frame from behind.
Equipment: 'A' frame and 2 hurdles.

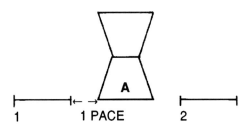

At first do this exercise with the jumps level with the foot of the 'A'-frame as shown in Figure 1. As the dog progresses, move them gradually nearer to the centre of the 'A' frame until you can do the exercise with the jumps as shown in Figure 2.

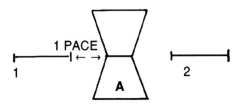

1. With the dog on the handler's left, do 'A', turn right and jump 2, then do 'A' again. (P & p)

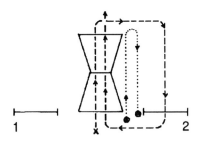

2. With the dog on the handler's right, do 'A', turn left and do jump 1, then do 'A' again. (P & p).

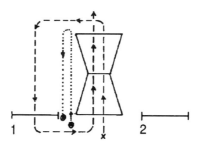

At first you will have to position yourself so that the dog goes round you to ensure a straight entry onto the 'A' frame the second time; but with practice, most dogs learn to straighten themselves.

When the dog can do this exercise with the jumps as shown in Figure 2 combine it with Exercise 1.

Exercise 4.

Aim of Exercise: practise turning into a tunnel from the 'A' frame and practise turning out of a tunnel onto the 'A' frame.

Equipment: 'A' frame and pipe tunnel set up as below.

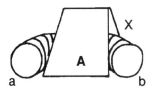

TUNNEL ENTRANCE &
EXIT ARE BOTH LEVEL
WITH ONE SIDE OF THE
'A' FRAME

FIGURE 1

1. Starting from X, do 'A' then tunnel from b. (P & p). See figure 1.

2. Starting from X, do 'A', then tunnel from a. (P & p). See figure 1.

Experiment to see which side you find it best to handle your dog for each of these.

3. Do tunnel from a, then send the dog straight over 'A'. (P & p). See figure 2.

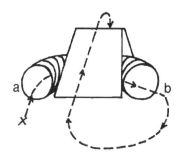

FIGURE 2

4. Do tunnel from b, then send the dog straight over 'A'. (P & p).
Later, combine stages 1 and 2 with stages 3 and 4.
5. Thus, starting from X, do 'A', then tunnel from b and send the dog back over 'A'. (P & p).
6. Starting from X, do 'A', then tunnel from a and send the dog back over 'A'. (P & p.)

Exercise 5.

Aim of Exercise: more practise of turning out of and into a tunnel under the 'A' frame.

Equipment: 'A' frame and tunnel. Practise both with the pipe tunnel and collapsible tunnel.

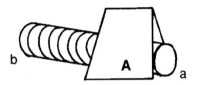

TUNNEL IS STRAIGHT & IN THE
CENTRE OF 'A' FRAME. ONE END
IS LEVEL WITH THE 'A' FRAME.

1. Do tunnel from a, then turn the dog right and do 'A'. The handler moves as shown below. (P & p).

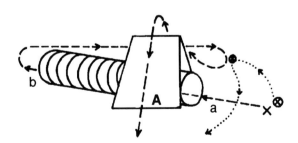

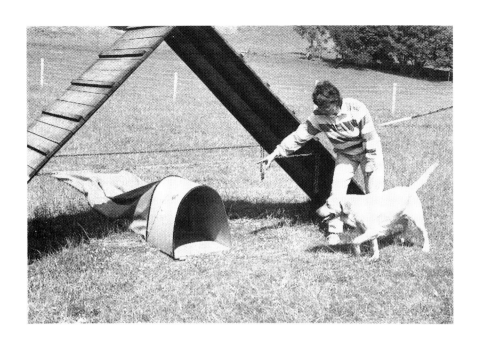

2. Do tunnel from a, then turn the dog left and do 'A'. (P & p).

When doing this exercise using the pipe tunnel, stages 1 and 2 can then be repeated doing the tunnel from b. This will give a sharper turn onto the 'A' frame.

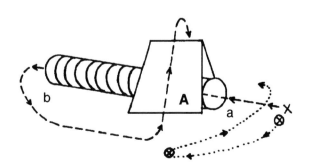

A lot of dogs will run past a tunnel when the entrance is just under the 'A' frame, so practise the following.

3. Do the tunnel from a. Turn the dog right and do 'A', then turn the dog left and the tunnel again from a. (P & p).

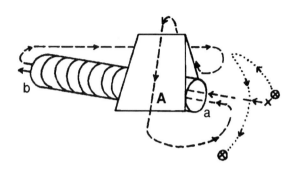

4. Do the tunnel from a. Turn the dog left and do 'A', then turn the dog right and do the tunnel again from a. (P & p).

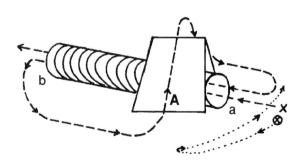

Exercise 6.

Aim of Exercise: to teach the dog to go up the 'A' frame from the opposite side to the handler.

Equipment: 'A' frame.

With some dogs it is possible to stand one side of the 'A' frame and send them to do the obstacle from the other side. This can be particularly useful in gambler classes.

1. Leave the dog at X and stand at Y. Call the dog over 'A'. (P & p).

2. Handler and dog both start at Y. Send the dog out to the left to the other side of the 'A' frame (P & p).

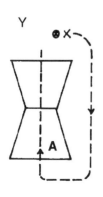

3. Handler and dog both start at Y. Send the dog out to the right to the other side of the 'A' frame. (P & p).

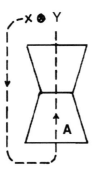

At first the handler will probably need to go half-way with the dog to help him. This exercise should only be done with the experienced dog who can straighten himself before doing the 'A' frame.

The handler goes half-way to help the dog.

Dog Walk

Exercise 1.

Aim of Exercise: directional control after the dog walk.

Equipment: dog walk and 3 hurdles.

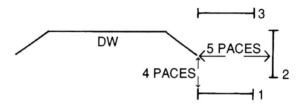

1. With the dog on the handler's left, do D. W., then send dog over jump 2, (p & p).

2. With the dog on the handler's right, do D. W., then send dog over jump 2, (p & p)

3. With the dog on the handler's left, do D. W. , command the dog to turn right and send him over jump 1. (p & p).

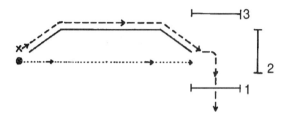

4. With the dog on the handler's right, do D. W., command the dog to turn left and send him over jump 3, (p & p).

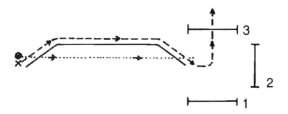

Exercise 2.

Aim of Exercise: directional control on to dog walk.
Equipment: dog walk and 3 hurdles set up as for Exercise 1.

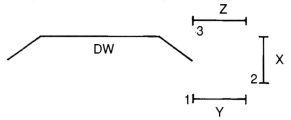

1. Leaving the dog at X, the handler stands by the start of D.W. Call the dog over jump 2, do D.W. (P & p).

2. Leaving the dog at Z, the handler stands by the start of D.W. Call the dog over jump 3, do D.W. with the dog on the handler's left. (P & p).

3. Leaving the dog at Y, the handler stands by the start of D.W. Call the dog over jump 1, do D.W. with the dog on the handler's right. (P & p).

By standing at the foot of the dog walk you are in the best position to ensure the dog steps on straight. At first, in stages 2 and 3, it may be necessary to step forward to prevent the dog stepping on from the side.

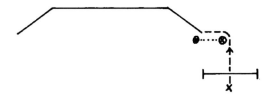

I find most dogs soon learn to straighten themselves before getting on, but the occasional dog will always need this help. When the dog is straightening without the handler's help, repeat stages 1 - 3 with the handler starting by the dog and letting him go ahead over the jump and onto the dog walk. The handler should then catch up, to ensure the dog gets the down contact.

Exercises 1 and 2 can then be combined in various combinations, such as:

1. Do D.W. Send the dog over jump 2, turn left and send the dog over jump 3, before doing D.W. again. (P & p).

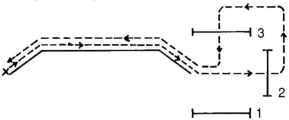

The handler lets the dog go ahead onto the dog walk.

2. Do D.W., send the dog over jump 2, turn right and send the dog over jump 1, before doing D.W. again. (P & p).

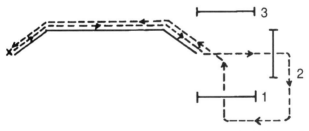

3. Do D.W. Turn the dog right over jump 1, then turn him left over jump 2, finally do D.W. again. (P & p).

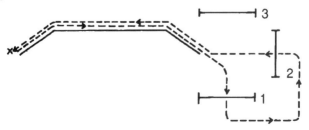

4. Do D.W. Turn the dog left over jump 3, then turn him right over jump 2. Finally do D.W. again. (P & p).

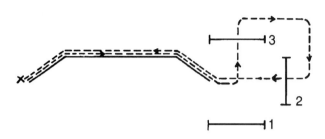

With more experienced dogs the handler should be able to stay in the middle of the jumps and not have to run right around.

Exercise 3.

Aim of Exercise: directional control on and off the dog walk.
Equipment: dog walk, pipe tunnel, 4 hurdles.

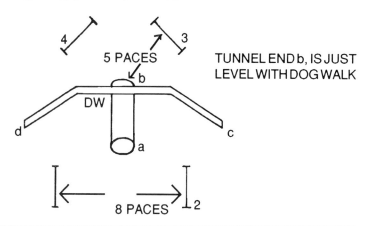

Care is needed when stepping over the tunnel.

Putting the tunnel under the dog walk like this is very useful for this exercise, but don't use it with beginner dogs unless the handler has long enough legs to step over the tunnel, so staying close to the dog on the dog walk.

Going out round the tunnel while the dog is on the dog walk may encourage a beginner dog to jump off.

Going out round the tunnel may make a dog jump off.

In this exercise be sure the tunnel stakes are not of the type that could injure the dog if he did jump off and land on one.

1. Start at X, do D.W. from c, turn the dog right and send him over jump 4, then do T from b. (P & p).

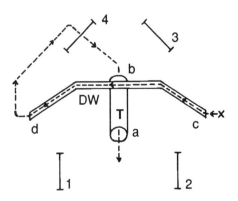

2. Start at X, do D.W. from d, turn the dog left and send him over jump 3, then do T from b. (P & p).

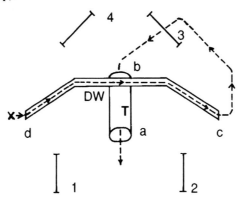

3. Start at X, do D.W. from c, turn the dog left and send him over jump 1, then do T from a. (p & p)

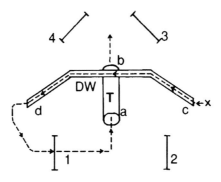

4. Start at X, do D.W. from d, turn the dog right and send him over jump 2, then do T from a. (p & p)

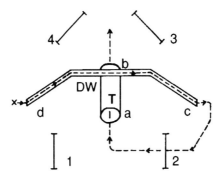

5. Start at X, do T from b, turn the dog right and send him over jump 1, then do D.W. from d. (P & p).

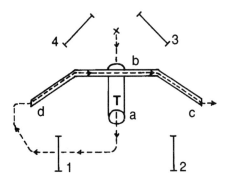

6. Start at X, do T from b, turn the dog left and send him over jump 2, then do D.W. from c. (P & p).

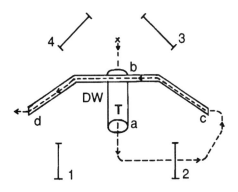

7. Start at X, do T from a, turn the dog right and send him over jump 3, then do D.W. from c. (P & p).

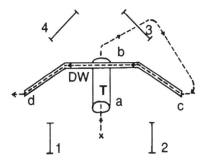

8. Start at X, do T from a, turn the dog left and send him over jump 4, then do D.W. from d. (P & p).

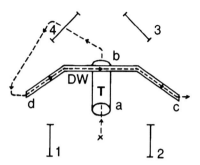

In stages 5 to 8 the handler should leave the dog at the tunnel entrance and step under the dog walk before starting. Be careful of your head. This set up is one I would never use in a competition because of the risk to the handler, but used with care it is a valuable training exercise.

Exercise 4.

Aim of Exercise: getting on to the dog walk from an awkward angle.
Equipment: dog walk and 1 hurdle.

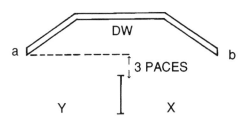

1. Leaving the dog at X, the handler stands at a. Call the dog over the jump and do D.W. (p & p)

2. Leaving the dog at Y, the handler goes and stands at b. Call the dog over the jump and do D.W. (P & p)

Do these two stages several times, helping the dog to straighten before the dog walk by taking a step forward and sending the dog round your leg.

Next repeat stages 1 and 2, the handler now running with the dog and beginning to send the dog on ahead to the dog walk.

Finally try stages 1 and 2 with the handler staying behind the jump until the dog is on the dog walk. Not all dogs will be able to do this.

If, at any time, the dog begins to step onto the dog walk from the side, go back to positioning yourself to straighten him.

Exercise 5.

Aim of Exercise: directional control out of the tunnel and onto the dog walk.
Equipment: dog walk and pipe tunnel.

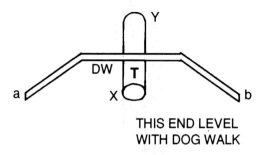

THIS END LEVEL
WITH DOG WALK

In the following, the handler should try to stay on the side of the dog walk where the exercise starts and move to the appropriate end of the dog walk as the dog turns out of the tunnel.

1. Start at X, do T. Turn the dog right and do D.W. from b. (P & p).
2. Start at X, do T. Turn the dog left and do D.W. from a. (P & p).
3. Start at Y, do T. Turn the dog right and do D.W. from a. (P & p).
4. Start at Y, do T. Turn the dog left and do D.W. from b. (P & p).

With the really experienced and keen dog, try standing at one end of the dog walk and send the dog past the tunnel entrance to the other end of the dog walk.

At first, stand half-way between the tunnel and the end of the dog walk (position X). Send the dog to the dog walk end a.

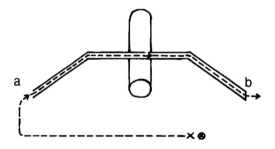

When the dog can do this from X, move slowly nearer to b until you can do it the whole way. Repeat this standing at a and sending the dog to b.

94

See-saw

With all the exercises using the see-saw the handler should try to ensure the dog gets both contact points and also tips the see-saw each time i.e. the see-saw should be touching the ground before the dog gets off.

Exercises 1 and 2.

Exercises 1 and 2 as given in the section on the dog walk should be worked through, replacing the dog walk with the see-saw.

Exercise 3.

Aim of Exercise: calling the dog to the see-saw and also sending him ahead to the see-saw.

Equipment: see-saw and 2 hurdles in a straight line.

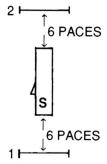

1. Running with the dog on the left send him over jump 1. Do S and finally jump 2. (P & p).

2. Repeat stage 1 handling the dog on the right.

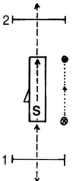

3. Leaving the dog at X, the handler stands on the right by the start of the see-saw. Call the dog over jump 1, do S and send the dog on over jump 2. (P & p).

4. Repeat stage 3 with the handler standing on the left of the see-saw.

5. Repeat stages 3 and 4 with the handler standing
at the end of the see-saw

6. With both handler and dog starting at X send the dog over jump 1 and onto the see-saw. The handler should then rejoin the dog to ensure he gets the contact and tips the see-saw. Finally, send the dog on over jump 2. (P & p).

Exercise 4.

Aim of Exercise: directional control before and after the see-saw.
Equipment: see-saw and 4 hurdles.

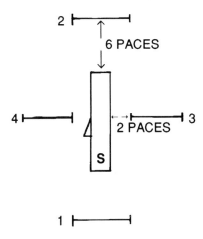

1. With the dog on the handler's left, send him over jump 1. Do S, then jump 2. Call
the dog back and send him over jump 3, then jump 1. (P & p).

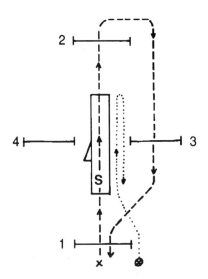

2. With the dog on the right, send him over jump 1. Do S, then jump 2. Call the dog back and send him over jump 4, then jump 1. (P & p)

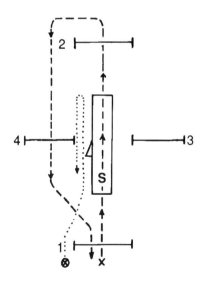

3. With the dog on the left, send him over jump 1. Do S, turn the dog right and send him over jump 3, then jump 1. (p & p)

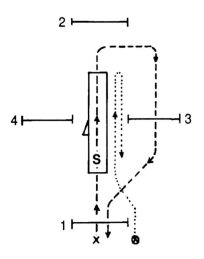

4. With the dog on the right, send him over jump 1. Do S, then turn the dog left and send him over jump 4, then jump 1. (p & p)

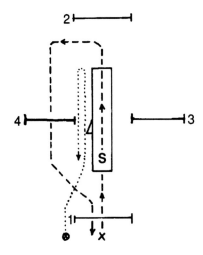

5. With the dog on the left, send him over jump 1. Do S, turn right and send him over jump 3, then do S again, and finally send the dog over jump 2. (p & p)

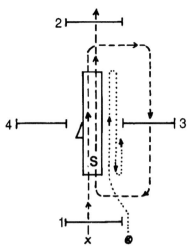

6. With the dog on the right, send him over jump 1. Do S, turn left and send him over jump 4, then do S again and finally send the dog over jump 2. (p & p)

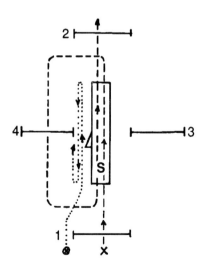

With stages 5 and 6, the dog is approaching the see-saw from an awkward angle the second time, and may need help to straighten before getting on. Don't allow the dog to step on from the side.

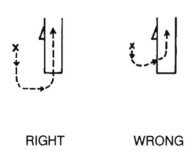

RIGHT   WRONG

The dog may need help to straighten up.

This exercise could be done with the handler leaving the dog at the start and standing by the see-saw, then simply moving along the see-saw as required. However, unless the see-saw was the second obstacle in a course, you would be unable to do this in a competition, so I feel it is of more value to send the dog ahead each time.

To vary this exercise, jumps 3 and 4 may be replaced by the two tunnels as shown below.

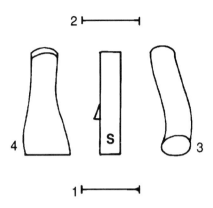

Tunnels can replace the jumps in this exercise.

Exercise 5.

Aim of Exercise: more directional control.

Equipment: see-saw and 5 hurdles.

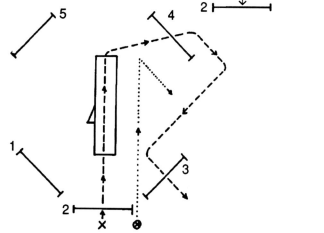

5 PACES

5 PACES

1. With the dog on the left, send him over jump 2. Do S then send the dog over jump 4, then jump 3. (P & p).

2. With the dog on the right, send him over jump 2. Do S, then send the dog over jump 5, then jump 1. (P & p).

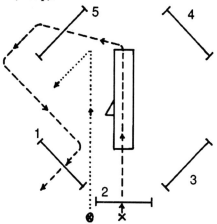

3. With the dog on the left, send him over jump 1. Do S, then jump 4, followed by jump 3. Then do S again and finally jump 5. (P & p).

The handler may find it easier to change to the other side of the dog as he goes up the see-saw the second time.

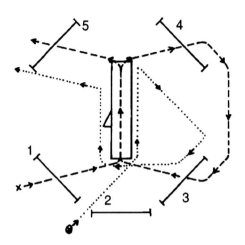

4. With the dog on the right, send him over jump 3. Do S then jump 5, followed by jump 1. Then do S again and finally jump 4. (P & p).

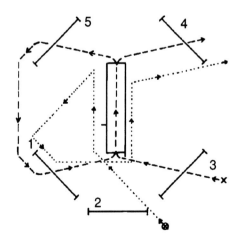

There are many other variations with this set up of obstacles. Also, turning the see-saw through 180° gives more variety.

Dog-cross

Exercise 1.

Aim of Exercise: directional control on the Dog-Cross and approaching it from different angles.

Equipment: Dog-Cross and 3 hurdles.

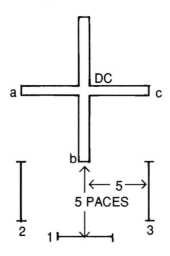

1. With the dog on the left, send him over jump 1. Do D.C. from b to c. Send the dog over jump 3 and do D.C. again from b to c. (P & p).

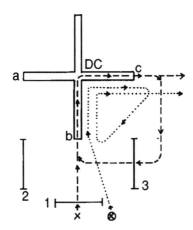

2. With the dog on the right, send him over jump 1. Do D.C. from b to a, send the dog over jump 2 and do D.C. again from b to a. (P & p).

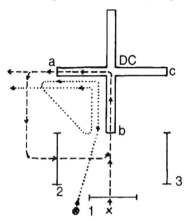

3. Leaving the dog at X, the handler stands in front of jump 2. Call the dog over jump 1. Send him over jump 2, then do D.C. from a to b and finally send the dog over jump 1. (P & p).

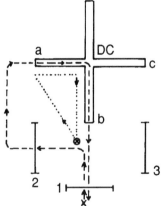

4. Leaving the dog at X, the handler stands in front of jump 3. Call the dog over jump 1 and send him over jump 3. Then do D.C. from c to b and finally send the dog over jump 1. (P & p).

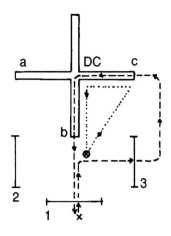

This exercise can be varied by using the pipe tunnel instead of jump 2 or 3. Also alter the position of the jumps to change the angles of approach to the dog-cross.

When the dog is proficient at this exercise try exercise 2.

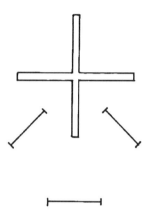

Exercise 2.
Aim of Exercise: directional control on dog-cross.
Equipment: dog-cross.

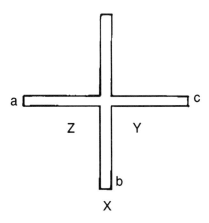

1. Leaving the dog at X, the handler stands at Y. Send the dog over D.C. from b to c. (P & p).

2. Leaving the dog at X, the handler stands at Z. Send the dog over D.C. from b to a. (P & p).

3. Handler stands at X. Send the dog up D.C. from b to c giving directional command just before the dog reaches the top and moving over to c as the dog comes down, ready to ensure he gets the contact. (P & p).

4. Repeat 3, but send the dog over D.C. from b to a. (P & p).

5. Leaving the dog at X, the handler stands at Z. Send the dog over D.C. from a to b. (P & p).

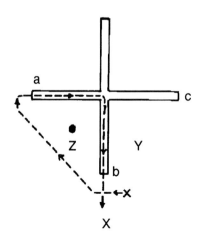

6. Leaving the dog at X, the handler stands at Y. Send the dog over D.C. from c to b. (p & p)

When the dog can do stages 5 and 6 try these two stages with the handler staying at X.

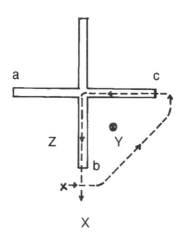

The handler now sends the dog to each plank.

Notes

9

OBSTACLE TRAINING USING TUNNELS AND THE TYRE

TUNNEL

It can save time in a competition if the dog comes out of the tunnel facing the direction he is next to go. Vital seconds are lost by the dog who circles, unsure of where to go next.

I find it quite possible to teach the dog to turn either to the right or left as he emerges from the tunnel. (Of course you also need to teach him to go straight ahead on command).

Most dogs turn naturally to the right and need more work to teach them to turn left. I always try to find out which way is natural to the dog before beginning to teach him to turn on command.

Finding out which way the dog turns.

To find out, stand directly in front of the tunnel and send the dog through. Stay still and don't give any command to the dog as he comes out. Repeat this several times. You will find most dogs will turn the same way each time, usually to the right.

With all the following exercises, do them using both types of tunnel whenever possible.

Exercise 1.

Aim of Exercise: teaching the dog to turn on command as he leaves the tunnel.
Equipment: tunnel and 2 hurdles.

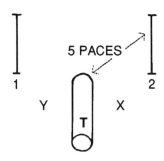

With this exercise, give the directional command while the dog is still in the tunnel; don't wait until he comes out. At first you may need to repeat the command as the dog emerges, particularly on the turn he finds most difficult.

1. With the dog on the left, do T, turn right and send the dog over jump 2. (P & p). Repeat several times.

2. With the dog on the right, do T, turn left and send dog over jump 1. (P & p). Repeat several times.

At first, help the dog as much as possible, perhaps by standing at either X or Y to warn him of which way he is to turn.

When the dog is used to the exercise, try to stay at the tunnel entrance and turn the dog by command alone.

Exercise 2.

Aim of Exercise: more practice of directional control out of the tunnel, now returning over the jump.

Equipment: tunnel and 2 hurdles.

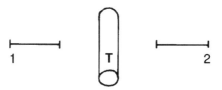

1. With the dog on the left do T, turn the dog right and call him back over jump 2. (P & p). The handler may need to move over as shown.

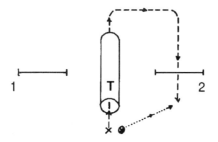

With the dog on the right, repeat stage 1, but turn dog left and call him over jump 1.

With an inexperienced dog the handler may need to run with the dog and send him over the jumps rather than call him.

Exercise 3.
Aim of Exercise: teaching the dog to turn or to go on ahead on command.
Equipment: tunnel, 3 hurdles, table.

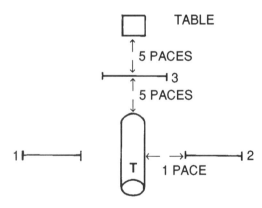

The table is added to this exercise to help the dog to go on ahead. He should be used to doing agility send away to the table ('*Agility is Fun*' Book 1, Jumping Exercise 4).

Repeat the stages of tunnel Exercise 2, but also send the dog straight ahead through T and over jump 3 to the table. 'Down' him for a few seconds and then use the opportunity to practise a recall over jump 3 and through the tunnel.

Exercise 4.

Aim of Exercise: practice of turning into a tunnel from different angles.
Equipment: tunnel and 3 hurdles.

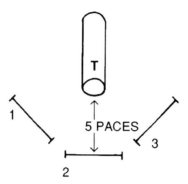

1. At first run with the dog, doing the tunnel after each jump.

When he can do this try to send him ahead over the jump and into the tunnel. Give the tunnel command as soon as the dog is committed to doing the jump.

2. Now move jumps 1 and 3 to make the angle of entry sharper and repeat stage 1.

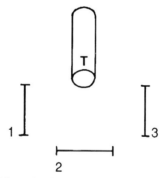

3. Move jumps 1 and 3 so the dog has to come back to the tunnel.

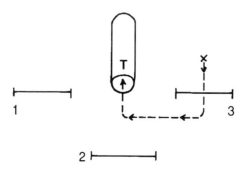

Exercise 5.

The previous tunnel exercises can now be combined to give many variations - these are just a few.

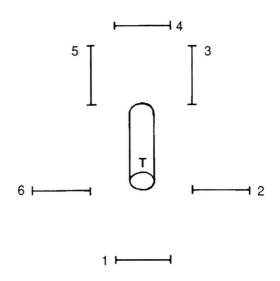

1. Send the dog over jump 1, do T, jump 3, then jump 2.
   Do T again, then jump 4. (P & p).
2. Send the dog over jump 1, do T, jump 5, then jump 6.
   Do T again, then jump 4. (P & p).
3. Send the dog over jump 1, do T, jump 4, then jump 3. Do T, then jump 1.(P & p).
4. Send the dog over jump 1, do T, jump 4, then jump 5. Do T, then jump 1.(P & p).
5. Send the dog over jump 1, do T, jump 3, then jump 2. Do T, then jump 5.(P & p).
6. Send the dog over jump 1, do T, jump 5, then jump 6. Do T, then jump 3. (P & p).

Exercise 6.
Aim of Exercise: directing the dog to chosen end of pipe tunnel.
Equipment: pipe tunnel and 2 hurdles.

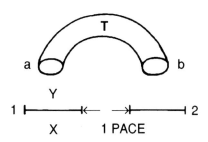

1. Running with the dog on the left, send him over jump 1. Do T from a to b, then send the dog over jump 2. (P & p).
2. Leaving the dog at X, the handler stands at Y. Call the dog over jump 1, do T from a to b, then send the dog over jump 2. (P & p).
3. Handler stands at X and sends the dog over jump 1 and through T from a to b, then moves across to call him back over jump 2. (P & p)..

Repeat stages 1 to 3 doing jump 2 first, the tunnel from b to a, then jump 1.

When the dog is happy with this, try using only one jump.

Doing jump 2 first.

120

Repeat the exercise using only one hurdle.

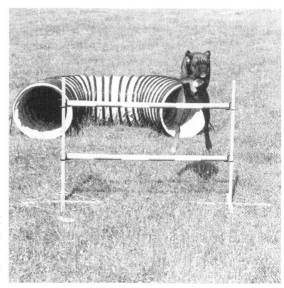

Giving the right or left directional command as the dog lands from the jump may help to send him through the chosen end of the tunnel.

Exercise 7.

Aim of Exercise: doing the tunnel only on command.

Equipment: both tunnels and 3 hurdles.

Many dogs love tunnels so much that their handlers find it difficult to pass a tunnel entrance on a course without the dog going through. This exercise should help.

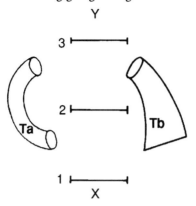

The hurdles are 6 to 8 paces apart, and the tunnel entrances are close to the side line of the jumps.

1. Running with the dog on the left, do jumps 1, 2 and 3, in order. (P & p).

2. Running with the dog on the right, repeat stage 1.

3. Leaving the dog at X, handler stands at Y. Call the dog over jumps 1, 2 and 3. (P & p).

4. Handler stands at X and sends the dog over jumps 1, 2 and 3. (P & p).

5. Running with the dog on the left, do jumps 1 and 2, then turn right and do Ta. (P & p).

6. Leaving the dog at X, handler stands on the right of jump 2. Call the dog over jumps 1 and 2 and send him on over jump 3. (P & p).

Standing in this position, the handler should be able to stop the dog from going through the tunnel as he did in stage 5.

7. Repeat stage 4.

8. Running with the dog on the right, do jump 1, then Tb. (P & p).

9. Leaving the dog at X, the handler stands on the left of jump 1. Call the dog over jump 1 and send him on over jumps 2 and 3. (P & p).

10. Repeat stage 4.

Tyre

Always put your dog straight at a tyre. You risk injury to the dog's back if he jumps through at an angle. Also once the dog is jumping the tyre at full height, never alter it.

Exercise 1.

Aim of Exercise: sending the dog on through a tyre and recalling through a tyre.

Equipment: tyre, table and 2 hurdles

1. Running with the dog on the left do jump 1, then T, jump 2, and put dog 'down' on the table. Keep him 'down' for several seconds, never let the dog jump straight off again. Handler goes to stand at x, recalls dog over jump 2 and sends him on through T and over jump 1. (P & p)..

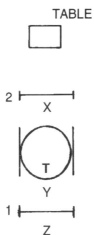

TABLE

2. Repeat stage 1 handling the dog on the right.

3. Run with the dog, do jump 1, then the handler stays at Y and sends the dog on through T, over jump 2 and onto the table. 'Down' for a few seconds. (P & p).

4. Following on from stage 3, handler stays at Y and recalls the dog over jump 2 and through T, then sends the dog over jump 1. (P & p).

5. Standing at Z, handler sends the dog over jump 1, through T, over jump 2, and 'downs' him on the table. After a few seconds, recall the dog over the obstacles. (P & p).

Some dogs will learn to do this exercise quickly, others will find it very difficult. Each stage should be perfected before attempting a harder stage, and the handler must always be prepared to go back a stage if problems arise.

When sending the dog on ahead, always be ready to re-join the dog if he stops. Try not to let him run back to you, rather run on with him for the rest of the way.

When recalling the dog through the tyre, try to keep eye contact through the hole, then he will be a lot less likely to run around it.

Try to have eye contact through the tyre.

A toy or titbit can be placed on the table to encourage the dog to go ahead, or an assistant could stand behind the table encouraging the dog.

Exercise 2.
Aim of Exercise: practice turning after a tyre.
Equipment: tyre and 2 hurdles.

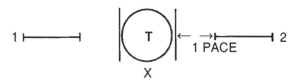

1. Stand at X, send dog through T, turn him right and recall him over jump 2. (P&p)

2. Repeat stage 1, but turn left and recall over jump 1. (P & p).

3. From X send the dog through T, then recall him between T and jump 2. (P & p).

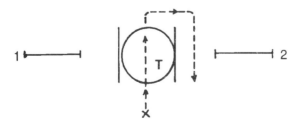

4. Repeat stage 3, but turn the dog left and recall between T and jump 1.
5. From X send the dog through T, then call him back through T again. (P & p).
Don't do stage 5 too often, or with a beginner dog.
This exercise can also be done using the well instead of the tyre.

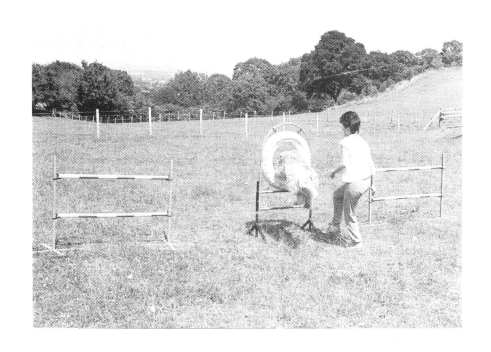

Exercise 3.
Aim of Exercise: directional control after the tyre, controlling the dog before it.
Equipment: tyre and 4 hurdles.

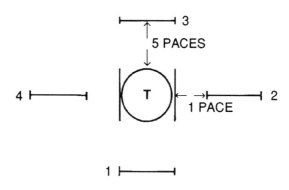

1. With the dog on the left send him over jump 1, do T, and jump 3, then turn right and do jump 2. (P & p).

2. With the dog on the right, send him over jump 1, do T, and jump 3, then turn the dog left and send him over jump 4. (P & p).

3. With the dog on the left do jump 1, and T, then turn him right and do jump 2, then jump 1. (P & p).

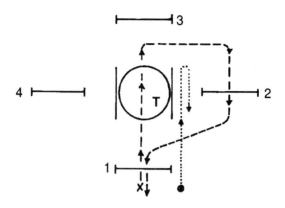

4. Repeat stage 3 but turn left over jump 4. (P & p).

5. Leaving the dog at X, the handler stands at Y. Call the dog over jump 1, then send him over jump 4, and running with him on the left, do jump 3, T, and jump 1. (P & p).

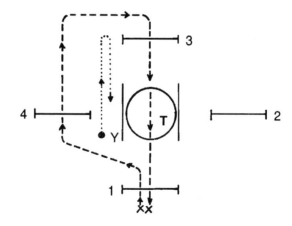

6. Repeat stage 5 but going the opposite way over jump 2. (P & p).

In stages 5 and 6 the handler should try to send the dog ahead from jump 3 to the finish.

Exercise 4.

Aim of Exercise: teaching the handler to straighten the dog before a tyre.

Equipment: Tyre and 2 hurdles.

Never do this exercise with a beginner dog. In competition a judge should ensure the dog has a straight approach to the tyre, but occasionally a judge does put a bad angle of approach in a course. I train handlers to straighten their dogs before doing the tyre using this exercise.

1. Leaving the dog at X, the handler stands in front of the tyre. Call the dog over jump 2, straighten him up round the handler and send him through T. (P & p).

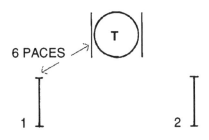

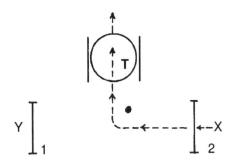

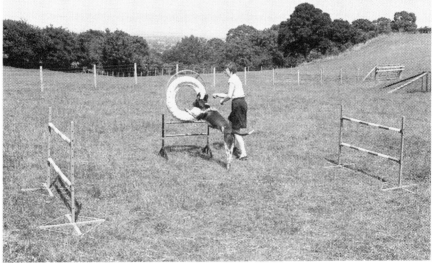

2. Repeat Stage 1 leaving the dog at Y and calling him over jump 1. When the handler is proficient at Stages 1 and 2 try Stages 3 and 4.

3. Handler and dog starting at X. Run with the dog doing jump 2, then T. (p & p) Steady the dog before T.

4. Repeat Stage 3 starting at Y.

With a very fast dog that gets ahead of the handler it may be necessary to 'down' him after the jump. Never just hope the dog will straighten up, a nasty bang on the back can really put a dog off tyres for a long time. If the handler cannot control the dog enough to do this exercise safely it should not be attempted.

Notes

10

OBSTACLE TRAINING WITH THE LONG JUMP AND THE TABLE

LONG JUMP.

Exercise 1

Aim of Exercise: directional control after the obstacle.
Equipment: Long jump and 4 hurdles.

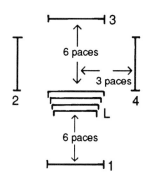

1. Running with the dog on the left, send him over jump 1, then L and jump 3. Turn the dog right and send him over jump 4, then jump 2. (P & p).

Be careful to take the dog far enough back behind jump 4 and straighten him before doing the jump or he may be likely to jump back over the long jump.

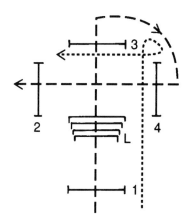

2. Running with the dog on the right, send him over jump 1, L and jump 3, then turn him left and send him over jump 2, then jump 4. (P & p).

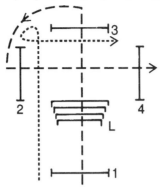

3. With the dog on the left, send him over jump 1, then L before turning the dog right and sending him over jump 4. (P & p).

4. With the dog on the right, send him over jump 1, then L, before turning the dog left and sending him over jump 2. (P & p).

Exercise 2

Aim of Exercise: sending the dog on over a long jump; recalling him over this obstacle.

Equipment: long jump, 2 hurdles and the table.

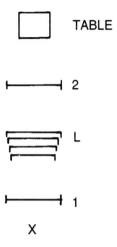

TABLE

|—————————| 2

L

|—————————| 1

X

1. Running with the dog on the left, send him over jump 1, L, then jump 2, finally 'downing' him on the table for a few seconds. (P & p)

2. Repeat Stage 1 handling the dog on the right.

3. Leaving the dog at X, the handler stands in front of L, calls the dog over 1, then runs with him doing L, jump 2, and onto the table. (P & p)

4. Leaving the dog at X, the handler stands behind L, calls the dog over jump 1 and L, then runs with him doing jump 2 and the table.

Do Stages 3 and 4 both with the dog on the left and with him on the right. Remember to leave him 'down' on the table for several seconds.

5. Leaving the dog at X the handler stands by the table, calls the dog over jump 1, L, then jump 2, and 'down' on the table. (P & p)

6. Leaving the dog at X, the handler stands in front of jump 2, calls the dog over jump 1, and L, then sends him over jump 2 and onto the table. (P & p) The handler remains behind jump 2.

7. Leaving the dog at X the handler stands in front of L, calls the dog over jump 1 and sends him on over L and jump 2, to the table. (P & p)

8. Starting at X, send the dog ahead over jump 1, L, jump 2, and onto the table. (P & p)

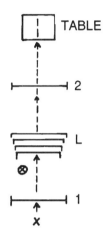

Exercise 3

Aim of Exercise: teaching the handler to straighten the dog before the long jump.
Equipment: long jump and 3 hurdles.

Most judges don't put bad angles of approach to a long jump but, as with the tyre, it is best to be prepared. I don't use this exercise with beginners.

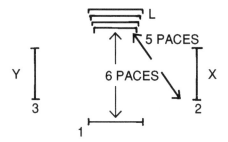

1. Leaving the dog at X, the handler stands in front of L. Call the dog over jump 2, straighten him around you, and send over L. (P & p).

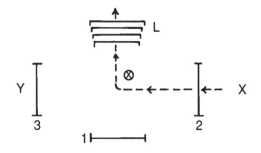

2. Leaving the dog at Y, the handler stands in front of L. Call the dog over jump 3, straighten him up and send him over L. (p & p)

When you can straighten the dog up like this try the following.

3. Running with the dog on the left, do jump 1, then L. Turn the dog right and do jump 2 before doing L again. (p & p)

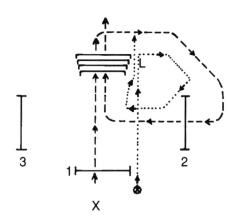

4. With the dog on the right, do jump 1, then L. Turn the dog left and do jump 3, before doing L again. (P & p).

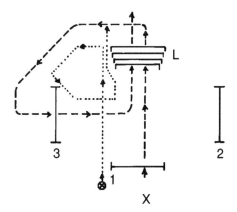

Table

Exercise 1

Aim of Exercise: directional control before the table.
Equipment: table and 3 hurdles.

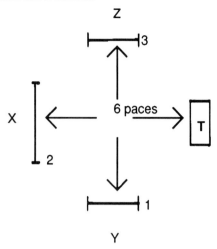

1. Running with the dog on the left, do jump 2, then T. (P & p).
2. Repeat Stage 1 with the dog on the right.
3. Repeat Stage 1 with the handler remaining at X.
4. Running with the dog on the left, do jump 1, then T. (P & p).
5. Repeat Stage 4 handler staying at Y.
6. Running with the dog on the right, do jump 3, then T. (P & p).
7. Repeat Stage 6, handler staying at Z.

Exercise 2

Aim of Exercise: send away to the table and pause box.
Equipment: table, 4 hurdles and pause box.

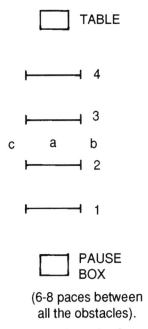

□ TABLE

⊢———⊣ 4

⊢———⊣ 3

c　　a　　b

⊢———⊣ 2

⊢———⊣ 1

□ PAUSE
　 BOX

(6-8 paces between
all the obstacles).

1. Run with the dog doing all the obstacles, going from pause box to table. (P & p).

Practise handling the dog on both sides. Repeat Stage 1 several times with the handler trying to stay further and further back until you can do this remaining by the pause box and sending the dog ahead.

2. Now starting from the table, teach the dog to go the opposite way, finishing in the pause box.

3. Leaving the dog in the pause box, the handler stands at a. Call the dog over jumps 1 and 2, then send him over jumps 3 and 4, to the table. (P & p).

4. Repeat Stage 3 working from the table to the pause box.

You may find Stages 3 and 4 are easier and can be done before the dog is able to be sent the whole distance.

5. Repeat Stages 3 and 4 with the handler standing at b.

6. Repeat Stages 3 and 4 with the handler standing at c.

7. Handler standing by the box. Send the dog over the jumps to the table, 'down' him for a few seconds, then recall him over the jumps. (P & p).

8. Repeat Stage 7, starting and finishing on the table.

Exercise 3

Aim of Exercise: practise of turning the dog to face the direction in which he will be leaving the table.

Equipment: table and 4 hurdles.

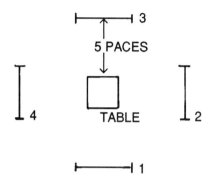

Each time the handler should make the dog face the direction in which he will leave the table, before 'downing' him. Make the dog 'wait' for several seconds on the table each time.

1. Send the dog over jump 1, then onto T and down, before sending him over jump 2. (P & p).

2. Repeat Stage 1, but leave T over jump 3. (P & p).

3. Repeat Stage 1, but leave T over jump 4. (P & p).

4. Repeat Stage 1, but leave T over jump 1. (P & p).

11
EXERCISES USING THE
WEAVING POLES

Once the dog has learnt to weave (see *'Agility is Fun'* Book 1 Chapter 9) every opportunity should be taken to practise.

Exercise 1

Aim of Exercise: to teach the dog to enter the poles correctly from different angles.
Equipment: set of weaving poles and 1 hurdle.

1. The hurdle, placed 4 to 8 paces from the poles, is moved around so that the dog enters from different angles.

Begin with the easiest.

At first leave plenty of room between the jump and the poles so the handler has time to position the dog before he enters the poles. Later move the jump closer and encourage the dog to enter the poles ahead of the handler.

Practise entry from this range of angles.

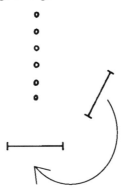

2. Now position the hurdle beside the poles as shown in diagram A.

The jump is about 2 paces out to the side of the poles. At first, the handler will need to help the dog to turn and line up ready for entry.

Vary the position of the hurdle, gradually moving it back, so making the angle of entry sharper. (Diagram B).

Diagram A

Diagram B

3. Repeat Stage 1 with the hurdle on the other side of the poles.

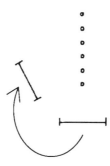

4. Repeat Stage 2 on this side.

With Stages 3 and 4 the dog has to learn to go round the poles before entry and will need quite a lot of help.

It takes a very long time to really perfect weaving and although I have put all these stages as one exercise, it will take several months to work through them. Although I said at the beginning practise the poles as often as possible, never let the dog get fed up, always keep weaving fun.

Exercise 2

Aim of Exercise: teaching the dog to enter the poles by himself.

Equipment: 2 or 3 sets of poles (4 to 6 in each), several hurdles.

Depending on the available space set up a circle of obstacles. Have 2 or 3 hurdles between each set of poles and no more than 6 poles in each set.

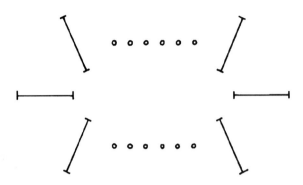

1.   Running with the dog on the left, do the obstacles in a clockwise direction. (P & p).

Repeat this stage several times with the handler beginning to hang back at the poles, so allowing the dog to enter himself. Always be ready to help if he gets into difficulty.

2.   Running with the dog on the right, try this in an anti-clockwise direction. The handler should encourage the dog to enter the poles ahead and then can drop in behind in their usual position for the poles (i.e. dog on left), changing back to having the dog on the right after the poles. Alternatively, the handler may choose to run all the way round with the dog on the left, obviously much further.

With a really experienced dog Stage 2 can be used to teach the dog to weave on the right of the handler.

Do this stage several times with the dog on the left at the poles, then begin to hang further and further back until the dog can complete the weaves with the handler in line.

When the dog is happy with this, begin to move nearer to the poles on their left side,

⊗ HANDLER STOPS HERE

until the dog is happy weaving with the handler on this side.

Some dogs accept this happily, others don't. I never feel it is worth messing up a dog's weaving to do it; but if you can teach this and still keep the dog happy, it is a big advantage when the weaving poles come in a left hand loop.

Exercise 3

Aim of Exercise: practise of the dog entering the poles ahead of the handler.

Equipment: set of weaving poles and 3 hurdles.

3 ⊢━━━━⊣   ⊢━━━━⊣ 2

```
                    o
                    o
                    o
                P   o
                    o
ABOUT 6 PACES       o
BETWEEN POLES       o
& HURDLES
```

⊢━━━━━⊣ 1

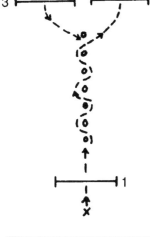

1. Leaving the dog at X, the handler stands by the entry to the poles, calls the dog over jump 1, does P, then jump 2. The handler turns the dog left and calls him back over jump 3, then does P and jump 1 again. (P & p).

2. Repeat Stage 1 but now the handler starts at X, sends the dog over jump 1 and allows him to enter the poles ahead. (P & p).

How soon the handler rejoins the dog after he has entered the poles will depend on each dog. Some are happy to do a complete set of poles alone, others will stop after 2 or 3 if the handler is not alongside.

When the dog is happy with Stage 2 repeat Stages 1 and 2 sending the dog over jump 3 and calling him back over jump 2. This gives a harder angle of entry into the poles.

Exercise 4

Aim of Exercise: directional control after the weaving poles.
Equipment: set of weaving poles, both tunnels and 1 hurdle.

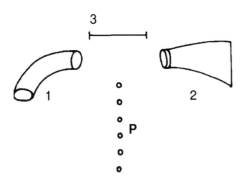

The tunnels can be replaced by hurdles

The tunnels can be replaced by hurdles but I find dogs often go wrong in the poles if they see a tunnel close by, so using them in this exercise is very good practice.

1. Do P, then send the dog over jump 3. (P & p).
2. Do P, then turn the dog to the right and do 2. (P & p).
3. Do P, then turn the dog to the left and do 1. (P & p).

This exercise can be varied by placing one of the tunnels at 3.

A tunnel is placed at the end of the poles.

Exercise 5

Aim of Exercise: directional control before and after the weaving poles.
Equipment: set of weaving poles and 6 hurdles.

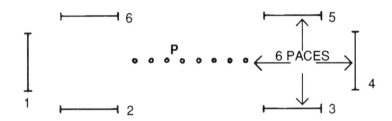

There are many variations possible with this set up. Here are three examples.

1. Send the dog over jump 1, do P, then jump 4 and jump 5. Do P again, then jump 6. (P & p).

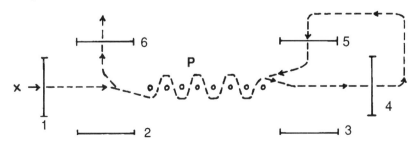

2. Send the dog over jump 2, do P, then jump 5 and jump 4. Do P again, then jump 1. (P & p).

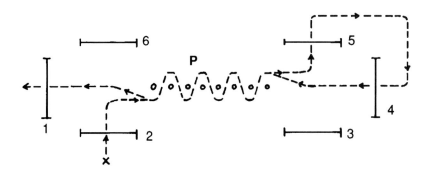

3. Send the dog over jump 6, do P, then jump 3 and jump 4. Do P again, then jump 2. (P & p).

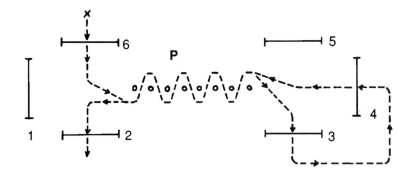

12
OBSTACLE AWARENESS EXERCISES

I do quite a lot of training where I put the dog in the position of having to make a choice of obstacles.

I find these exercises really teach the dog the obstacle commands and make him listen to his handler.

The most common 'choice' situation met in competition is the 'A' frame and tunnel (number 1 below). I also use all the other obstacles in many different combinations.

Here are a few examples.

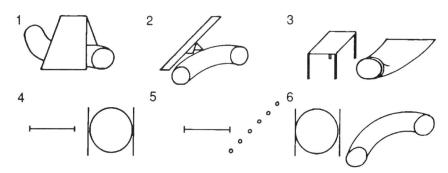

Set up the chosen two obstacles very close together. Remember your obstacle command is the name of the obstacle to the dog, e.g. if you use 'through' for tunnels, a tunnel to the dog is a 'through'.

Showing the dog the correct obstacle.

Stand about two yards away from the obstacles and start with the obstacle the dog likes least. Give a firm command and make sure the dog does the correct obstacle, either by holding his collar, or by blocking the other obstacle with your body. Repeat in this way several times.

Next, use the same obstacle but now send the dog ahead of you.

When the dog is doing this correctly, go on to the second obstacle of the pair. Work on this obstacle in the same way as the first, but remember the dog has got used to doing the first obstacle and you may have to work harder to make him do the right one.

Getting the dog up the 'A' frame.

Finally, alternate between the two obstacles.

When doing this kind of exercise there are three important points to watch.

1. Always give the obstacle command clearly and early enough. Give it 2 yards away and repeat it at the obstacle. It is unfair to leave giving the command until the dog is right up to the obstacle.

2. Praise the instant the dog has made the right choice, e.g. when he puts his foot on the 'A' frame. The only exception to this is the tunnel. Wait until he exits from the tunnel before praising or he may turn round and come back out of the entrance.

3. Never tell the dog off for making the wrong choice. You don't want to put him off an obstacle. Instead, simply don't praise him if he goes wrong but make him do the correct obstacle straight away. Make sure, by holding him if necessary, that he does the right one. Then give lots of praise.

When the dog gets proficient at this type of exercise, put a jump in front of the choice and send the dog over this first. Remember to give the choice command as soon as the dog is committed to doing the jump.

Later you can use three different obstacles.

156

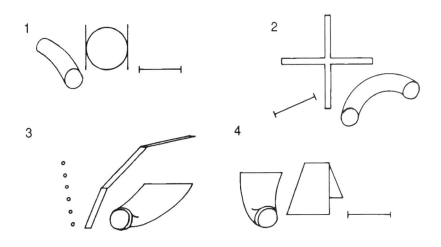

When the dog really knows the commands and is listening to you, set up a short course which includes a choice e.g.

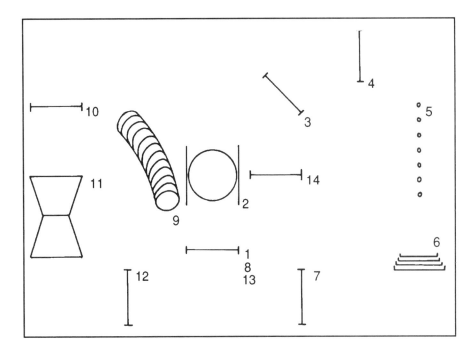

Notes

13

PROBLEMS

Once you start competing regularly and your dog gets more experienced and confident in the ring, you may find problems repeatedly cropping up that you need to cure.

In this chapter I have listed some of the various problems that arise and suggest some tips that may help you solve them.

CONTACT POINTS

Contact points cause most of us problems at sometime. Many beginner dogs go well down the contacts at first, then as they get more and more confident and keen, they start to jump off. So what can you do if this happens? Here are some suggestions to try.

1. 'Downing' the dog.

I don't think there is any way you can explain to a dog that jumping off 1" above the coloured area is wrong, yet 1" below is right. So I believe in training the dog to go as far down the contact as possible. I also believe that the reason most dogs miss contacts, is because they are in such a hurry to get to the next obstacle. So, in training, I always 'down' the dog at the bottom of the contact and make him wait, then praise him for waiting and continue.

If the dog gets used to expecting a 'down', he is less likely to leap off.

Downing the dog after the contact.

2. Using your hands.

Many handlers use their hands to try to position their dogs on the contacts. Either pointing down or trying to make the dog go under their hands.

This may be successful but I find that often the dog sees these hands as an obstacle to jump over, so be sure you are not holding your hands in the wrong position.

When using their hands I encourage handlers to stand at the side, not at the foot of the contact, with their back to the way they will be going.

Standing at the side you are still able to line yourself up for the next obstacle and the dog is less likely to set off in the wrong direction.

3. Titbits.

Holding a titbit in your hand (in training only) and giving it at the base of the contact, or placing one at the base, will work with a few greedy dogs who are ever hopeful of a tasty morsel. However, the majority of dogs quickly realise you don't carry titbits in the ring and so this is not effective.

4. Making the dog 'wait' on the obstacle.

Either on the top of the 'A' frame or on the down plank of the dog-walk. (The 'wait' on the see-saw is a different matter and I shall deal with that separately).

I think it is a good thing to teach any dog to 'wait' on the 'A' frame or dog-walk but it doesn't necessarily always help with the contact problem.

With very fast, keen dogs, making them 'wait' can sometimes make them more impatient and more inclined to jump off.

If you do make the dog 'wait' on the obstacle, the place where you stop the dog is important. On the 'A' frame you want the dog to stop at the apex, but if his back feet have gone over the top before he gets the 'wait' command, most dogs will find it impossible to stop. So on this obstacle give him the command before he's gone over the top and hopefully, he will stop on the top.

On the dog-walk I find the nearer you can let the dog get to the contact area before stopping him, the better. On this obstacle I find it is really better to work towards being able to steady the fast dog over the whole obstacle, than stopping him.

5. Making the dog 'wait' before starting the obstacle.

This I have found a lot more effective than actually stopping the dog on the obstacle.

You can either 'down' or 'sit' the dog before the obstacle, or simply make him wait in the stand. At first you may need to do this on the lead so that you can be sure of stopping the dog. Make him 'wait' for a few seconds, then praise (for waiting) before allowing him to do the obstacle.

When doing this, the place where you stop the dog is very important as you don't want to risk him putting a foot on and off the obstacle. (Thus getting a refusal). Also very important when doing this off the lead: if the dog does get away from you and starts up the obstacle, let him carry on over, don't call him back. You don't want to encourage the dog to turn round on contact equipment. If he does go right over after ignoring your 'wait' command, simply take him back and ensure he 'waits' next time, using the lead if necessary.

Teaching the 'wait' before a contact obstacle has two advantages: it gives you the time to get into a good position to ensure the dog gets the contact, and also, because the dog has stopped, he will be less likely to tear over the obstacle.

Of course, how much you make your dog 'wait' when competing depends on the dog. A steady dog may not need it at all; a slightly faster one may just need a 'steady' command as he comes up to the obstacle; a very fast, keen dog may need to be actually stopped before doing the obstacle.

6. Changing where you stand.

I find if you hang back, particularly at the 'A' frame, rather than getting ahead of the dog, his attention will be on you and not on the next obstacle and so he may come further down the contact.

The handler hanging back may help.

7. Changing your command.

If the dog is persistently missing contacts, re-train him using another command.

8. Put a tunnel at the foot of the contact.

This should be about 1 yard away. The dog's gaze is brought down to the tunnel and, hopefully, his feet as well. This works well in training but, unfortunately, most dogs realise they won't find a tunnel in this position in the ring.

This works well in training.

9. Using training hoops.

These are hoops that can be fixed in the ground at the start and finish of each piece of contact equipment.

I have found these hoops very useful when first training a young dog as you can teach him to go right down the contact without stopping. However I have not found them very successful in the re-training of an experienced dog. They may work in training but the dog knows only too well that he won't find them in competition.

Before using hoops with the equipment teach the dog to go through the hoops alone using the command you use to try to keep the dog on the contact, rather than using a through command.

Training hoops used with the 'A' frame.

I have found with contact points that even if you think you have found a cure, after a few weeks or months of success the problem may come back. You always have to be prepared to try something different.

Unfortunately I believe there is no foolproof. If anyone has one I would be delighted to hear about it!

Training hoops used with the Dog Walk.

Training hoops used with the Dog Walk.

THE SEE-SAW

The training tips suggested for the 'A' frame and dog-walk apply to the seesaw as well, but here we meet another problem: the dog that 'flies' off the seesaw. This is a very annoying fault and can be dangerous to the dog who could get hurt.

On this obstacle I believe in training the dog to 'wait' in the centre until the seesaw has tipped. In training I always exaggerate this 'wait', keeping the dog still until the plank has been on the ground for a few seconds. I then let the dog walk down and make him 'lie down' on the plank and praise him while he is still 'down'. In this way you teach the dog to come down the plank in a crouching position, which makes it harder for him to 'fly' off.

Usually it is the fast, nutty, dog that 'flies' off the

see-saw. Steadying him, or even stopping him in the 'down' before the obstacle, may be necessary. Never let this type of dog rush on to the next obstacle. In training 'down' him and praise him for waiting before continuing.

MISSING THE UP CONTACTS.
'A' frame

German Shepherds seem most prone to this, often jumping right over the contact area.

I have found the best way to cure this problem is to place titbits on each of the up side slats and teach the dog to climb up collecting them.

Dog walk and see-saw.

On these occasionally a dog begins to step on from the side so missing the up contact.

To cure this I use two rows of poles to form a kind of wing. I never use proper wings as they could encourage the dog to jump.

The dog climbs up collecting the titbits.

The poles form a wing.

JUMPING FAULTS.

Knocking fences down.

Any dog, particularly a fast one, can mistime a jump, but if your dog is persistently knocking fences down, you need to think hard about the reason.

Firstly, is the dog overweight? If so it's hardly fair to be jumping him. Lose some weight off the dog (fast road-work is excellent for this) and the jumping problem may be solved.

Secondly, is the dog's sight all right? If you have any doubt a visit to the vet may help.

If neither of these is the problem, is it a young dog that has been over-faced with full height jumps too soon, so lacks confidence? If this is the case, a week or two jumping lower height jumps may get back the dog's confidence and cure the problem.

How is the dog knocking the fences down? In this series of photos, the dog has taken off far too soon and probably didn't realise this was a spread until too late, so he comes down on the back pole.

Here the dog's take-off is at fault. In fact, often a poorly timed take-off is the problem, and can be caused by the handler giving the command in the wrong place.

As an agility handler, you have a lot to think about when controlling your dog. Where to go next, what traps to avoid, getting short of breath, etc. So it's no wonder you don't always give the command at the right moment.

With many dogs this doesn't matter, they won't take off until they are ready, regardless of when you give the command. But many other dogs jump immediately they get the command and then you get problems.

I'm a great believer in making the dog think for himself and not telling him when to take off. A dog that thinks about his take-off is a lot more likely to time it right than one who relies on his handler to tell him when to jump.

Of course the handler still directs the dog and gives encouragement. With my Collies I command them to go on if the jumps are in a straight line, or give them the directional commands if they have to turn. The only time I use the 'up' command is if my dog is at a stand-still right under a jump.

So if you are having a problem with your dog consistently knocking fences down, it might be worth 'shutting up' yourself and getting the dog to think for himself. How do you do this?

The dog must be experienced enough to know that jumps are for jumping. This is not for a young dog just beginning agility.

Put up a straight row of five or six jumps (about 6 paces apart) and try running with the dog, without giving the 'jump' command. Give whatever command you use to send the dog on and use your hand to show him the jumps if necessary.

If your dog refuses to 'jump' do the row a few times using the 'jump' command, before trying it without.

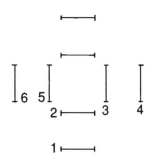

Once the dog is doing a row like this happily, change the distances between the jumps, so now he really has to think. Keep altering the distances, sometimes have a really long gap and even have one occasionally just slightly less than 4 yards.

When the dog is coping well with this straight line, put jumps at the sides and get the dog used to turning.

1. With the dog on the handler's left, send him over jumps 1 and 2 using the command to send the dog straight ahead (I use the command 'go on'). As the dog lands after jump 2, give him the command to turn right, then after jump 3, command him to go straight on over jump 4.

2. With the dog on the handler's right, send him straight on over jumps 1 and 2, then command him to turn left for jump 5, and straight on again for jump 6.

If after trying this your dog still cannot get his take-off right, experiment with a white pole on the ground in front of the jump. Using this you can encourage the dog to take-off nearer to, or further away from the jump as necessary.

Experiment with a ground line.

170

With an experienced dog who persistently knocks fences down and doesn't seem to care whether he jumps the fence or barges through it, I suggest verbally telling the dog off after he's knocked a fence down. Growl at him and even pick up the pole and show him it saying, "What's this" in a gruff voice. Then do the same jump again with lots of praise if he clears it.

Getting a friend to stand by the jump holding the pole and raising it to **lightly** touch the dog as he jumps, may also help but be careful not to put the dog off jumping; only just touch him, never hit the dog.

I believe many dogs get blase always jumping 2'6", so if the dog is capable of the extra height, I often put several jumps up to 2'9" in training. I find this makes the dog think more about the jumps. (I would never alter the height of the tyre).

Running past jumps

If your dog repeatedly runs past jumps, he may have been over-faced doing full height too soon. I find, even with dogs well capable of jumping 2'6" early in their training, it is much better to get the control and confidence over lower (probably 2') jumps before doing much at full height.

Get the dog confident over lower jumps.

With a dog that is likely to run past a jump, keep him close to you on the approach to the jump and really line him up with the centre before telling him to jump. You may find it helps to stay behind the jump until the dog has done it. If you run round he will be inclined to follow.

Going under single pole jumps

I like to train all dogs to jump single poles. In fact, with experienced dogs, I do most of my training with single poles. However, how you introduce the dog to jumping single poles is important. The method now described can also be used to re-train a dog who keeps going under the poles.

First, get the dog really used to jumping a line of 3 jumps, each with at least 3 poles on, and well spaced at about 6-8 paces. Get the dog used to working on both sides of the handler.

When the dog is happy with this, lower the height of the jumps to 2' (lower with very small dogs). Remove the lower poles, one at a time, until the dog is jumping the 2' high hurdle with only a single pole.

Teaching the dog to jump a single pole.

Again practise working the dog on both sides and also making him 'wait' and then recalling him over one or two jumps.

After a lot of practice at this height, start to slowly raise the height, only 1" at a time, getting the dog's confidence at each height, until 2'6" is achieved.

When the dog is really confident with single pole jumps, put a tunnel in the line of jumps and practise this. Many dogs run under a single pole if they see a tunnel is next.

Spread jumps

If taught correctly (see 'Agility is Fun' Book 1, Chapter 10) spreads should not cause any real problems.

A smallish dog, such as a Sheltie, will find a full-sized spread (2' if parallel, 2'6" if the front pole is lower than the back), difficult, and the handler must ensure this type of dog has a good, straight, run at a spread.

Using a different command just for spread jumps may help as it warns the dog that he must make an extra effort even if he cannot see the back pole before take-off. Adding to your 'jump' command may also help e.g. saying 'get up', 'big jump' or 'right over'.

Banking the wall and the well

I like a dog to be really confident at full height jumps before he tackles a wall; also confident with spreads, before tackling the well, as this is so inviting to bank (stand on).

If the dog does start to bank the wall, try putting a white pole on the ground in front, to give a ground line. Also try getting a friend to hold a pole just in front of the wall a couple of inches below the top line. I find this will usually make a dog clear the wall.

To stop the dog banking the wall.

With the well, I find placing a number of loose poles on the body of the well, so that the dog who stands on the well will tread on these, this usually cures the problem quickly. The poles move when the dog stands on them, usually making quite a 'clatter' and most dogs do not like this. So next time they jump through cleanly.

.Another possible cure for banking the well is to hold two white poles, one either side to make the well into an ascending spread. A ground line may also help.

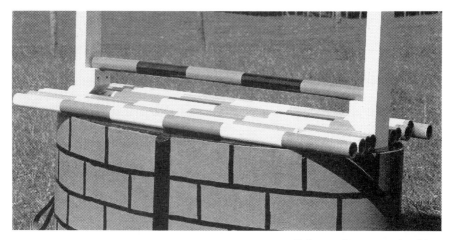

Poles to discourage banking.

Making the well into an ascending spread.

Long jump

Many dogs get careless with this obstacle and start to clip the last board. A few training sessions with a hurdle in the middle, as used when introducing a dog to the long jump, usually makes the dog jump higher and so cures the problem. A dog who walks the planks needs re-training with them on their edges and a hurdle. (*'Agility is Fun'* Book 1, Chapter 9).

The hurdle makes the dog jump higher and longer.

THE TYRE

I think the tyre is potentially the most dangerous obstacle on an agility course. If the dog mistimes it or jumps through at an angle, he can easily bang his back and be put off tyres for a time. He may also start jumping through the side or going under suspended tyres, or just running past.

Care when first introducing the dog to tyres is essential (see *'Agility is Fun'* Book 1 Chapter 9) and the beginner dog should always be taught the correct hole to jump through.

If problems do develop, careful re-training may be necessary.

Running under a suspended tyre.

It may only be necessary to get someone to hold a pole across the gap a few times but if the dog reverts to running under as soon as the pole is removed, try the following.

Put the dog on the lead (using a plain collar not a check collar) and walk quietly up to the tyre, holding the dog so he can't go through or under. Show him the hole under the tyre. Let him put his nose through, then check him back and say 'No' very firmly. Do this two or three times, then show him the correct hole and praise him lavishly for showing interest in this hole; not necessarily jumping through, although obviously you don't stop him if he does want to jump.

Now take him back and quietly approach the tyre again with the dog still on the lead.

Give your tyre command and show him the correct direction. If the dog jumps through, let go of the lead (so you don't check him) and praise with great enthusiasm.

Repeat this several times, checking any attempt by the dog to go underneath. Then try it off the lead, going back to the lead if the dog goes under again.

This method can also be used to stop a dog who runs through the side of a suspended tyre.

Check him back and say'No'.

Show him the correct direction.

176

Running past the tyre.

Adding jump wings either side for a while may help this problem, or re-train on the lead as above.

While having any problem with the tyre, care should be taken to approach tyres with the dog under control and close by your side. In competition, take the time to point out the right way. If the dog still runs past, it may be best to sit him in front of the tyre and go round and call him through to you, again showing him the correct direction with your hand. Always remember to praise for success.

Call the dog through the tyre.

TUNNEL
Turning back on entering.

If the dog is persistently turning back blocking the entrance to prevent his happening is essential. The handler can then concentrate on calling and encouraging the dog from the far end.

Blocking the entrance with a solid board or door that excludes light is in my opinion cruel, especially with beginner or timid dogs.

I have a specially made heavy gauge wire door which can be fixed to the tunnel entrance when needed.

This method can also be used for dogs that dislike entering wet tunnels.

A solution to the tunnel problem.

Fouling the tunnel.

This is a problem you must deal with immediately it happens.

Using a very deep gruff voice leave the dog in no doubt of your extreme disapproval. Remember to thoroughly cleanse the tunnel afterwards so no scent remains.

TABLE

Running underneath.

This quite often happens when the obstacle before the table is either a tunnel or the see-saw. The dog's attention is down on the ground and he may not see the table in time to jump up onto it.

Teaching the dog a 'table' command, as opposed to using your 'jump' command, helps here because the dog associates the 'table' command with a higher than usual jump (most tables being over 2'6"). As long as the command is given early enough, his attention is directed upwards before he reaches the table.

'Downing' the dog on the table.

This can be a real problem with some dogs and I've seen handlers going to great lengths trying to get their dogs to lie down on the table.

If re-training is necessary, go back to first principles. On the lead, work on getting an instant 'down' on the ground. Praise quietly when this is achieved, using the voice alone, as you shouldn't touch your dog on the table. When you can do this well on the lead with the dog beside you, progress to working off the lead and letting the dog go ahead of you before you 'down' him.

Use a pause box and keep the dog 'down' for at least 10 to 15 seconds each time. At first stand still while the dog is 'down'. As he improves, begin to walk about a bit. Go over to another obstacle and back while the dog is 'down'. Don't forget to praise each time.

Once the dog is good on the ground try using a low table - the mini table is ideal - before using the proper table.

Now use a low table.

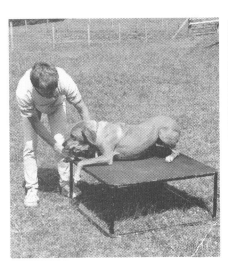

Changing your command when re-training for the table may also help, e.g. using 'flat' instead of 'down'.

I've also found banging the side of the table, or your leg, with a rolled-up newspaper as you give the command, can help to reinforce it in training. In competition this can be replaced by a loud clap.

WEAVING POLES

Wrong entry.

It takes quite a long time before a dog becomes reliable at entering the poles by himself, and with a beginner dog I always feel it is better to waste a second or two getting the dog in the correct position, than just to send him into the poles hoping for the best.

Practice is very important with weaving. The more times you can do the poles in training, the better. Practise entering from different angles. The exercises in Chapter 11 are designed to help to perfect weaving.

Once your dog is weaving really well, you may think your problems are over and they may well be, but, the occasional dog who has been weaving well will suddenly, for no apparent reason, begin to make mistakes. These are the most common mistakes, with some suggestions to try to cure them.

Entering the wrong side of the first pole.

With a dog that is persistently doing this, I put one wire from the first to the third pole, bent outwards so it doesn't stop the dog weaving correctly. This wire should be fixed at a height where the dog will run into it if he tries to enter wrong. Experiment to get the height right. Many dogs enter the poles with their heads low down, and you may find you need the wire quite low.

The wire ensures correct entry.

With this wire fixed, practise sending the dog into the poles from every different angle. You may need to keep this re-training up for quite a while, and in competitions the handler should make the dog 'wait' before the poles and show him the correct entry position, rather than risk him getting it wrong. Every wrong entry makes re-training harder.

Entering past the second pole.

This is quite common with very fast dogs who overshoot the poles. Steadying this type of dog before entry may be all that is needed, but a wire can again be used. This time it is fixed from the second to the fourth pole.

Now the wire is fixed from the second to the fourth pole.

Missing the last pole.

This often happens when the poles are followed by a tunnel, or when another obstacle is very close to the poles and attracts the dog's attention.

The collapsable tunnel may distract the dog from the poles.

Practise all these situations in training.

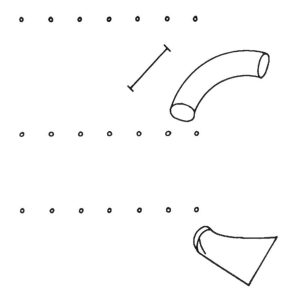

I find it often helps in situations like these to keep the weave command quiet at the start and centre of the poles, and make it more pronounced at the end.

Practise weaving with different numbers of poles, some dogs get used to doing 9 or 10 and go wrong when they meet 11 or 12.

Occasionally, in training, put out more than 12 and practise a really long weave.

Experiment to see whether the dog is more likely to miss the last pole with an odd or an even number of poles. With an odd number the dog finishes towards the handler, with an even number he goes away. This can be significant; if so, you can be prepared and may be able to prevent the fault with your voice.

Missing poles.

This is very common with the fast, excitable, dog. Try to steady this type of dog before he enters the poles and keep your commands calm all the way through.

Experiment to see whether the dog goes better with you behind or in front of him.

With the persistent offender I have found it is best to practise first with just a few poles, perhaps only 5. Do these lots of times, maybe putting them in a simple course, and giving quiet praise whenever the dog completes them successfully. When 5 have been mastered, increase the number, one at a time, until the dog is doing a whole row. Don't be tempted to rush this increase. Make sure the dog is proficient at lower numbers first.

Practise first with just a few poles.

The very slow weaving dog.

Exercise 2 Chapter 11, can be used to try to speed the dog up in the poles. Give lots of praise each time.

Using a titbit may help, although most dogs know they won't get one in competition.

I find having a toy in your pocket and throwing it upon completion of the poles, works well with some dogs.

Your most important aid is your voice. You want to make it sound really excited and enthusiastic, so the dog begins to think the poles must be worth doing after all.

It can be really hard work speeding up a dog in the poles, it won't happen over night but it is possible, so don't be put off trying.

Notes

14
PROBLEM DOGS
DOGS THAT BARK, BITE, AND JUMP UP

These are problems which should never have been allowed to develop in the first place. Teach 'quiet' as a command when the dog is young and make it mean just that. When you begin agility training stop any barking as soon as it starts.

However, this doesn't help if you have an older dog who persists in barking in agility. Uncontrolled barking often goes hand in glove with jumping up and even biting at the handler. I am now going to suggest a few tips which may help with any of these three problems.

When trying any of these suggestions, set out a very simple course, possibly just a circle of obstacles, so that you don't have to think where to go next. This will cut out any hesitation on your part.

1. With most of these dogs it is excitement that makes them bark and jump up. As soon as the dog barks, stop, put him in the 'down' position, and make him stay there until he's quiet and calm, then carry on. Repeat as often as necessary.

Keep the dog down until he is quiet.

187

2. When the dog barks, stop doing agility, put the lead on and do fast heel-work in and out of the obstacles.

If the dog still jumps up or bites, take hold of him by the scruff of his neck and give him a shake, growling at him at the same time. Then carry on with the heel-work. Get the dog doing fast heel-work without barking and biting, before recommencing agility.

For this method to work, it is essential to stop doing agility the moment biting or jumping up starts. Don't carry on hoping it won't get too bad. The dog must not be allowed to get away with a single bite. Don't shout when telling the dog off or putting him down, keep your voice quiet and low. Shouting will only excite the dog more.

3. Have a rolled up newspaper in your hand and slap it against your leg (not the dog). This makes a lovely noise and is very effective with some dogs.

4. Carry a squeezy bottle full of water and squirt the dog in the face when he barks, this works well with dogs who dislike water.

5. With a dog who loves agility, stop, put the lead on, and take him off the course. Leave him for half an hour or so before trying again.

6. If the dog bites at your arm, keep hand signals to a minimum and don't move your arms more than necessary. Also wear tight clothing, not clothes that flap around inviting the dog to grab hold.

7. Train over lower jumps for a while, the dog will not be so excited and this may help.

Squirt the dog with water.

With all these problems be consistent in your re-training. Never let the dog get away with it, always take some action. Finally, and very important, don't forget the praise when you've got the dog quiet and calm.

The dog which lacks enthusiasm

This type of dog often sniffs the ground a lot, star-gazes on top of the dog-walk and 'A' frame, runs off to see what other dogs are doing, and generally doesn't pay attention to his handler.

The handler who has this sort of dog often has poor basic control. If this is the case, short stretches of fast heel-work around the obstacles, done first on the lead and later off, should help. Keep the sessions short and work on keeping the dog's attention all the time.

Have a game and use lots of praise.

At the finish of these sessions, have a game with the dog and give plenty of praise. Using a squeaky toy, or occasionally giving a titbit, can help with this exercise. I'm not too keen on carrying the toy or titbit in the hand as it can encourage jumping up and biting. I find it better to keep them in a pocket where you can get at them quickly when necessary.

When doing this heel-work, use plenty of sharp turns but don't insist on precision obedience heel-work. In agility you want the dog to run happily beside you without getting under your feet. Slight deviation from your side doesn't matter, and nagging an under enthusiastic dog will only make him worse.

Try to fit in a short stretch of this agility heel-work in each training session, before you start on the obstacles. As well as helping to get the dog to pay attention, it is an excellent way to warm up both dog and handler.

The following exercises may help the under enthusiastic dog.

Set up a very simple exercise (such as either Exercise 1 or 2), and do it several times, giving lots of praise each time.

Exercise 1.

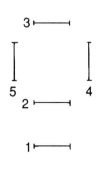

HURDLES ABOUT
6 PACES APART.

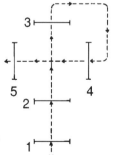

1. Do all the jumps in order 1 - 5.

2. Do this in reverse 5 - 1.

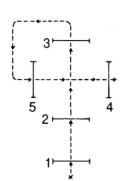

3. Do the jumps in this order 1, 2, 3, 5, 4.
4. Do this in reverse 4, 5, 3, 2, 1.

Exercise 2
1. Do jumps in order 1, 2, 3, 4, 5.
2. Do jumps in reverse order 5, 4, 3, 2, 1.

Find out where you lose the dog's attention. It may be on the turns, if so, use your voice to try to get a quicker response.

Although I suggest doing this sort of exercise several times. Be careful not to bore the dog. Having a game with a toy between each go often helps to keep it fun.

3. Teach control using lower jumps. Not having to worry about the height can give the dog more confidence. Sometimes a dog who lacks enthusiasm is one who has been over-faced with full height jumps before he was ready. A few weeks of jumping the lower height may help a lot.

4. Find out which obstacle the dog really likes and use it often. e.g. if the dog likes the pipe tunnel, set up a course like this.

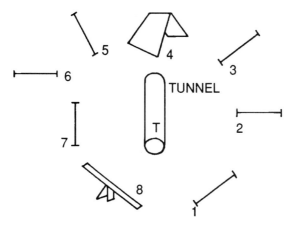

Practise combinations such as : 1.T.3.2.1.T.4.5.6.T.3.T.1.8.7.T.

5. When doing a course in training, watch the dog carefully and, as soon as he begins to lose enthusiasm, stop and have a game. Then restart the course a couple of obstacles back and carry on.

6. Set up a straight row of obstacles and try to race the dog.

7. Do a line of two or three obstacles and then throw the dog's toy.

With all these, keep the sessions short and fun. Don't be self-conscious, really play with the dog and be very enthusiastic with praise.

When competing, always have a game before you run, so the dog is happy at the start. Also, have a game when you finish the round, even if it wasn't so good

This type of dog is very hard work but it is very rewarding when he does discover *Agility is Fun* and begins to enjoy himself. Remember the most important thing is to keep it fun.

The over enthusiastic dog

This is the 'nutty' dog, usually very fast and noisy, who often circles a lot and rushes off to do his own course. He frequently knocks fences down and has no regard for contact points. Warm-up heel-work done round the obstacles can help this type of dog, as well as helping the under enthusiastic type. Do it first on the lead. Try to keep a steady pace when passing jumps, tunnels, etc. and check any attempt by the dog to do them.

Use a quiet, firm, voice and try to stop any jumping up, barking or biting by the dog. A small squeezy bottle of water can be very helpful in stopping the dog who jumps up. A small squirt of water in the dog's face often works wonders.

When you can complete the above type of heel-work on the lead without the dog trying to do any obstacles, try it off lead. Now you have only your voice with which to control the dog. Keep calm and resist the temptation to raise your voice. I find that even very 'nutty' dogs respond better to quiet commands than to shrieks, which only seem to excite them more.

A short session of this agility heel-work before you start obstacle training will help to calm the dog down as well as warm up you both.

Once you start work on the obstacles you must try to keep this type of dog under control. Here are a few suggestions to try.

1. Do a course, but make the dog lie down before each obstacle. Keep him in the 'down' for a few seconds, then praise him and do the obstacle. Always remember the praise. Only do a round like this once in a training session; if you do it too often it makes the dog frustrated.

When you can successfully complete a course with a 'down' between each obstacle, progress towards making the dog 'wait' before each. Do not necessarily make him go right down.

If the dog defies you and refuses to wait, take hold of him quietly and use your voice to scold him before trying again. If he still defies you, you may have to resort to using the lead for a time. Remember the praise when he does wait, it should come before doing the obstacle, as the praise is for waiting.

2. With a dog who persists in doing one particular obstacle e.g. the tunnel, try the following. Run with the dog by your side up to the obstacle in question (in this example the tunnel entrance). Then call the dog to heel and turn him away from the obstacle, sometimes turning to the right, sometimes to the left. If necessary, do this on the lead to begin with. Occasionally, stop the dog just before the obstacle and make him 'wait' before doing the obstacle. At other times, make him 'wait', then call him away from the obstacle. By doing this, the dog is never sure whether he's going to do the obstacle or not. This helps him to learn to listen to your commands.

3. Do a whole round, but miss out every other obstacle.

4. Divide a course into sections. Work on one part at a time, making certain the dog is getting it right before carrying on to the next section.

5. Teach the dog to listen to your commands. I find the best way to do this is to put the dog in the position of having to make a choice. The exercises and method of doing this are covered in Chapter 12.

6. When training this type of dog and making him 'wait' or 'down' before obstacles, always reward him by letting him fly round a simple bit of the course after. Don't frustrate the dog by stopping him all the time. e.g. set out this simple course opposite.

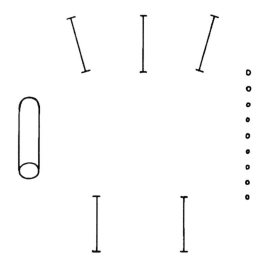

Now work through the following:

    a. Run the dog in a clockwise direction.

    b. Make the dog 'wait' between each obstacle.

    c. Repeat Stage a.

    d. Put the dog into the 'down' after each obstacle and walk on to the next before calling him.

    e. Repeat Stage a.

    f. Miss out every other obstacle.

    g. Repeat Stage a.

The whole exercise could later be repeated, working in an anti-clockwise direction.

7. Experiment with your commands. With some dogs, using their name before a command is a waste of time and breath. Others respond to their name very quickly. The name, when used, should be short.

8. Always be early with your commands. Tell the dog where to go next while he is in the air over the jump. Don't wait until he has landed and is halfway to the wrong obstacle.

An over enthusiastic dog is very hard work, but usually can take a lot of training quite happily. Once you get this type of dog under control he is a joy to work.

Dogs that only make mistakes in competition.

Most dogs are more excited when competing than when training at home, and handlers find they need to run and think faster in a competition than in training. Although faster in competition, the majority of dogs still react in the same way to different situations and problems can be sorted out in training at home.

However, a few dogs get so excited that they react differently in competition and make mistakes that they never make in training.

With this type of dog, if you don't get to grips with the problem where it arises (i.e. in competition) you will never cure it.

I know a lot has been said about 'no training to be allowed in the ring', but surely it is wrong to let a dog tear round out of control, knocking fences down and flying off contacts. I still maintain that with this type of dog you must work at controlling him during competition and be prepared to throw away a few classes to hopefully cure the problem.

What can you do during competition? Obviously you must not waste the judge's time, but quite a lot can be done in the normal amount of time you'd spend on a course. Any action has to be quick and effective.

If your dog has missed one contact and is likely to miss the next, why not handle the dog down the contact and be sure of getting it? You'll get 5 faults for handling, but you'd get 5 for a missed contact anyway. Or 'down' the dog before the next contact and try to take him over very steadily. I hate to see a dog rush round missing all the contacts without the handler taking any action.

If your dog rushes his fences and is knocking them down, make him 'wait' in front of a couple as you complete your round.

Don't let a fast dog rush onto the next obstacle; try to control him between the obstacles.

If you get eliminated and are allowed to continue or even have picked up 5 or 10 faults and know you won't be placed, don't waste the rest of your round. Try out things e.g. if you are not confident working your dog on both sides, now is the time to try.

Gambler classes can be used to advantage. You have 40 or so seconds to choose your own obstacles. You may be able to sort out a problem under competition conditions. Pay on the Day classes are also excellent for this.

Whether you call this 'training' or 'working' your dog in the ring, I'm sure the majority of judges would much rather see a dog being controlled than watch one defying his handler and running out of control.

Notes

15
OBSTACLE BUILDING

Many of the people who have been on agility courses with me have expressed interest in the equipment that I use, much of which is designed to help in the teaching of the complete beginner.

I find my adjustable height 'A' frame and dog walk very useful. They were designed and made by John Coleman who has kindly drawn the plans and written the instructions for construction that follow. He also gives instructions for building a seesaw.

To make obstacles, a reasonable competence of D.I.Y. is necessary. This is assumed, so some finer points are omitted. Any suggestions made can be modified.

Possession of, or the services of a welder, electric or gas, is essential to make variable height obstacles such as an 'A' frame and dog walk.

Wood alone can be used, but the finished obstacles are not as durable, and are heavier and more cumbersome.

Although sizes are mentioned, these are optimum and can be varied according to supply.

You may be lucky and know a second hand metal stockist who can supply all shapes, sizes and lengths of metal. Failing that, careful planning is necessary as metal is sold by the length, which may be 18 feet to 22 feet, and you could end up with a lot of off-cuts.

Use galvanised nuts and bolts of appropriate lengths and galvanised washers where the nut is to be secured onto wood. Also use galvanised nails.

All bare wood should be treated with a preservative. Also, treat wood surfaces which will be near or in contact with the ground. Allow to dry before priming. On metal, use a metal primer.

When selecting wood try a builders' merchant. Look at the stack of wood; if it is unduly rough, knotted, twisted or warped, beware and go elsewhere.

Try to select wood that is straight and not splintery or too knotted. Ideally the end grain should be vertical and parallel, thus:

 NOT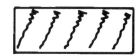

When joining wood to wood, some form of joint is advisable, but the more wood taken away, the weaker the product. No elaborate carpenter's joints are necessary, but having said that, the neater the joint the more pleasing the product. The choice is yours, chunky or neat.

Use an adhesive for all wood joints, both for strength and to keep the water out.

A builders' merchant should be able to supply all the wood requirements. Most wood is sold as "sawn". However the merchant should saw wood for you e.g. 4" x 2" into 2" x 2" and put it through a planer. The merchant should also supply the nails, nuts, bolts, washers and wood preservative, possibly some useful hints as well.

'A' FRAME.

'A' frame set low for the beginner.

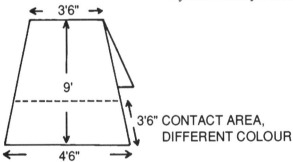

3'6"

9'

4'6"

3'6" CONTACT AREA,
DIFFERENT COLOUR

Metal is the only material which will allow the framework to be varied in height and will fold flat for storage and transport.

Most important for success is selecting the tube for the apex, this acts as the hinge and the struts onto which the wood cladding is bolted. Ideally select a 2" diameter tube, not thin walled, and another tube that will fit snugly inside it, both 3'6" long.

For the struts, angle iron can be used, but not deeper than 1 ¼" for a 2" tube, or metal with a cross section as below. Again, no deeper than 1 ¼". Each strut to be about 8'9" long.

The apex tube acts as a hinge.

Decide whether to use boards or plywood sheets as cladding. Bearing in mind that an 8' x 4' sheet will not clad one side, so a joint is inevitable, while boards, bolted together, can be replaced individually as required.

Using boards as cladding, 4 struts on each side would make a strong lasting job.

Assuming 4 struts on each side, cut the 2" tube into 8 x 3" lengths and 3 x 6" lengths. Cut with a hacksaw as a pipe cutter will burr the inside and the inner tube may not fit.

Assemble these lengths onto the inner tube thus:

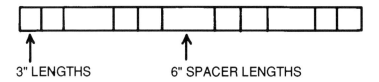

3" LENGTHS   **6" SPACER LENGTHS**

The 3" lengths have the struts welded to them, but note that the struts are not exactly opposite to each other, this allows folding.

Lay out the work for welding as follows, cladding side downwards.

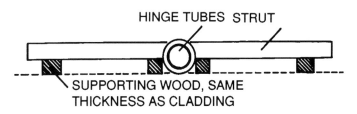

HINGE TUBES STRUT

SUPPORTING WOOD, SAME
THICKNESS AS CLADDING

PLAN VIEW

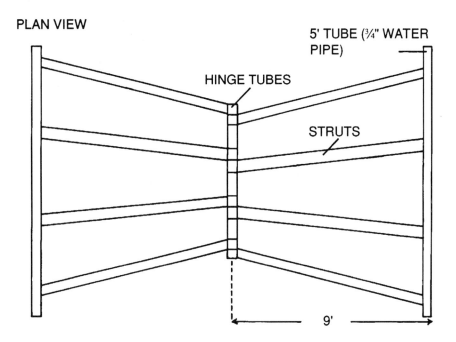

The 5' tube at the ends of the struts will, of course, protrude beyond the cladding. This will allow the 'A' frame to be pegged down if necessary.

The struts must be splayed to support the cladding evenly. Tack-weld the struts to the tubes and base tube. Remove inside hinge tube, turn each half over and weld each joint, then turn back again and finish the tacked welds.

Reassemble with centre tube. Use grease when inserting. Now drill a hole right through each outside spacer length and insert either a long split pin or a small bolt. This will stop the inner tube coming out.

The frame is now ready for cladding. Start at the base and work upwards. Use galvanised nuts and bolts.

The top board must be chamfered to fit with no gaps thus:

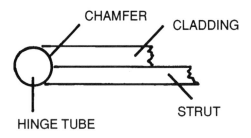

To make the height variable, drill holes in the outside struts, about 2' from the ground. Using D shackles and chain the proper height (6'3") can be achieved. Moreover, by drilling a second hole just below one of the holes and using more chain the frame can be opened out to lower the height for beginner dogs.

Use about 12' of 1" welded chain (not sheet linked chain) each side. Using 3 D shackles each side, the apex can be lowered by removing the shackle from the hole in the strut, but not from the chain so it stays in the appropriate link to re-erect to the 6'3" height.

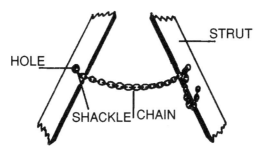

Use 1 ⅜" x ¾" lathes for anti-slip slats. 1 ¼" x ½" door stopping hardly gives enough grip. The lathes may need planing.

Slotted angle iron can be used to make an 'A' frame but it is only a second best, although no welding is needed. 8' x 4' plywood is best used for cladding, which means the base is only 4' wide, not 4'6".

The hinge would be just bolts through the slots of the angle iron at the apex, bolting each pair of struts.

The major problem with this construction is the gap at the apex. The only practical solution is a tube that will lie on this gap, slightly wider than the apex and held in position by two tensional springs. These springs are hooked into holes drilled into the tube at one end and onto a slot of the angle iron at the other.

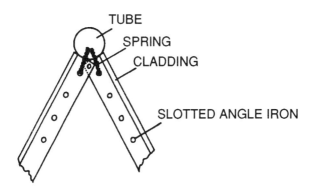

DOG WALK.

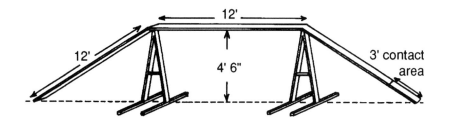

The dog walk set low for beginners.

To make a dog walk adjustable for height, two similar frames must be made, each consisting of one pair of legs, a frame to pivot the legs and bolt onto the horizontal plank, and half of the hinge for the inclined plank, the other half being bolted to the inclined plank.

First select 3 planks - 12' minimum 14' maximum length, 9" or 10" wide and 1 ¾" thick.

To construct the horizontal plank frame, take 2 lengths of angle iron 1½" or 1¾" x 14" long. Place them on a flat surface, parallel, angle upwards, the distance apart of the upwards angle just less than the width of the plank. Weld 2 pieces of 1" flat iron across onto the horizontal angle, flush at one end and 2" from the other end.

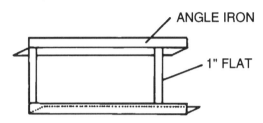

Weld a piece of angle iron, the width of the plank, to the frame, to look like this:

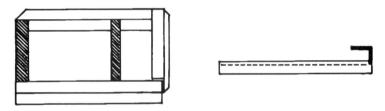

The end of the plank has to fit under the lip of the angle iron so weld to cater for this. A neater job is made if the level of the angle iron is the same as the board, by cutting out a slice of the top plank.

To make the hinge, select a piece of tube ½" internal diameter and a piece of rod that fits snugly into it. Cut 2 x 1 ½" lengths of tube and weld onto the angle iron as shown below, making sure the top of the tube is level with the top of the angle iron.

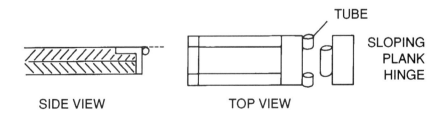

To make the other half of the hinge for the inclined plank, cut a piece of angle iron the same width as the plank. Weld a length of the tube that fits between the 2 tubes on the other half of the hinge, level with the top of the angle iron. To complete this half of the hinge, cut a piece off the end of the inclined plank so that the level of the angle iron and the plank are the same. Then weld 2 x 9" lengths of ¾" or 1" flat iron to the bottom of the angle iron so they run back along the lower side of the board. This will give the incline plank hinge lateral strength, especially when moving. How and where precisely the flat iron is welded onto the angle iron depends on the thickness of the board and depth of angle iron.

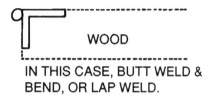

IN THIS CASE, BUTT WELD & BEND, OR LAP WELD.

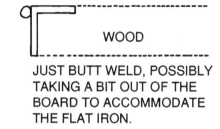

JUST BUTT WELD, POSSIBLY TAKING A BIT OUT OF THE BOARD TO ACCOMMODATE THE FLAT IRON.

At the ground end of the incline board nail a strip of galvanised tin, just narrower than the board, long enough to cover the butt end and about 6" up each side. Then with the rounded side of a hammer tap the edge of the tin all the way round to round it into the wood and prevent rough edges.

Use 1¼" x ½" planed door stopping for anti-slip slats and drill before nailing about 12" apart, not within 6" of start of contact point.

Use thinnish ¾" tube for the legs, 4 lengths of 54" and 2 lengths of about 36" to ensure stability of the legs.

At one end of each leg (54") weld a 1" length of ½" tube - this makes the hinge. Flatten the end of the ¾" tube a bit to make a neat weld.

The result to achieve is this: 2 pairs of legs hinged at the top which will fold together and pivot on the horizontal board frame.

LAID OUT FLAT.

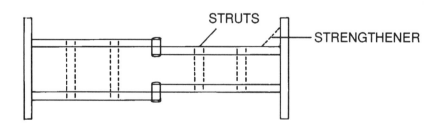

STRUTS

STRENGTHENER

SIDE VIEW, STANDING.

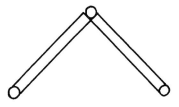

The distance of the legs apart is governed by the width of the board and frame. The hinge of the legs must fit snugly between the angle iron of the frame on the horizontal board. Thus:

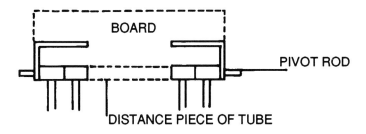

Weld 2 struts of flat iron to each pair of legs on the outside of the tube so as to allow the legs to shut together. The lower struts must not be opposite each other when shut for the same reason. Weld supports to the legs and stabilisers using flat iron.

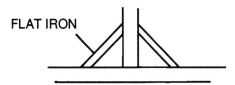

Drill the holes for the pivot rod in the horizontal board frame in such a position that the legs will fold as flat as possible along the underside of the board (for storage and transport) i.e. as far as is practical from the board.

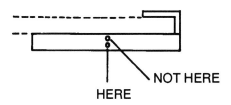

Lastly, a 6' piece of ¾" link or 1" link welded chain must be attached to the lower struts of the legs. Either buy or make a threaded eye for one strut and a threaded hook for the other strut.

Open the eye, put the end link of the chain on and shut it again.

Drill a hole in the middle of both lower struts. Bolt the eye into one hole. Bolt the hook into the other incorporating the other end link of the chain. This will stop the legs opening too far and the whole obstacle collapsing.

Now set up the obstacle so that the walk is 4'6" above the ground (maximum height), mark the link now on the hook, this saves a lot of time when readjusting the height. Similarly other links can be marked for different heights for training.

The whole obstacle can be constructed of wood, but it is heavy and cumbersome. However, if wood is your only medium it is better than no dog walk at all.

Use 2" x 2" wood for the legs and stabilisers. The comments made about measurements for metal legs apply to wooden legs too. For all but the hinging at the apex, use strap hinges and attach the butt end to a length of 4" x 2", the same width as the horizontal plank. Remember when calculating the width of the widest pair of legs that the butt of the hinge must not protrude beyond the end of the 4" x 2" on which they are attached. Keep the strengthening supports short or they may trip up the handlers.

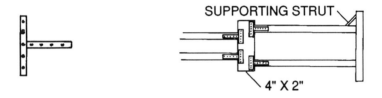

SUPPORTING STRUT

4" X 2"

The 4" x 2" and legs will have to be bolted to the horizontal board.

The leg assembly will have to be removed for transport so drill the holes for the bolts a little on the sloppy side, which will make removal easier. Chain assembly as for metal legs.

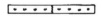

Strap hinges should be used for attaching the inclined board to the horizontal board. Use 2 and fit them on the upper surface, countersunk so they are flush with the surface of the wood. Use galvanised bolts as the sloping boards will also have to be removed for transport. Undercut the ends of both boards.

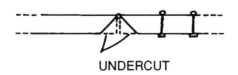

UNDERCUT

SEE-SAW.

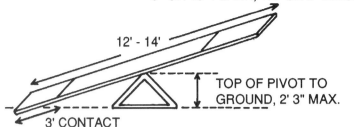

9" OR 10" PLANK, 1¾" OR 2" THICK

12' - 14'

TOP OF PIVOT TO
GROUND, 2' 3" MAX.

3' CONTACT

The base is two triangular constructions, wide enough apart to take the plank without being sloppy, the apex being the pivot position.

The frame can be made of either angle iron (1" or 1 ¼") or tube (¾") or a combination of the two.

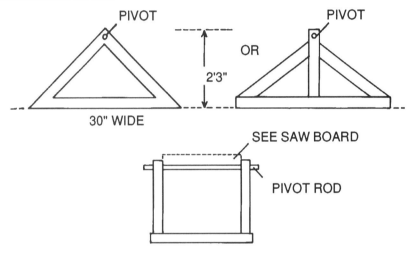

PIVOT   PIVOT

OR

2'3"

30" WIDE

SEE SAW BOARD

PIVOT ROD

If the pivot is made of angle iron, it must be heated and the two angles shut together, before welding the frame together, so that a hole can be drilled through it to accept the pivot rod. If tube is used it makes a neater job to flatten it, at the pivot.

To make a frame to bolt onto the seesaw board pivot, take a piece of tube, the width of the board, that will accept a ½" or so rod without being sloppy.

To this tube weld 4 pieces of 1" flat, about 9" long.

Lay out for welding on a flat surface thus:

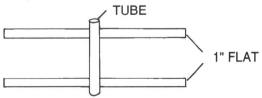

TUBE

1" FLAT

205

Weld, then turn over and weld the other side, making sure before welding that it is all on the same flat plane. Grind off any proud weld and bolt to the middle of the board. Drill the frame for the pivot rod. Drill also each end of the pivot rod to accept a split pin to retain the rod.

Edge each end of the plank with galvanised tin as for the dog walk.

Use 1 ¼" x ½" door stopping (planed) for anti-slip slats, drilling before nailing to avoid splitting. Test assembled seesaw for balance. It may need additional weight for your requirements.

When making the frame of wood, the same measurements would apply as for metal, but the design with a vertical centre piece would be best.

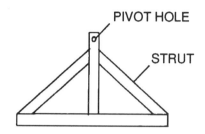

To accommodate the pivot rod on the seesaw board, bolt to the middle a piece of wood, a similar width and thickness about 10" long. Drill a hole through this for the pivot rod.

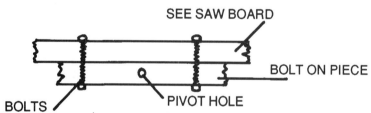

Better still use a suitable piece of pipe. Shape the bolt-on piece to accept the pipe, then bolt onto the seesaw board. Do not cut into the seesaw board itself.

Keep the pivot greased.

206

CONCLUSION

In this book I have assumed that the reader is familiar with the basics of Agility described in *Agility is Fun* and have covered the more advanced control work necessary for success in competition.

I have tried to prepare the handler for most eventualities but inventive agility dogs often manage to come up with the unexpected, spoiling what would otherwise have been a brilliant round.

In this 'if only' sport of ours, it is vital to keep your sense of humour at all times. Our dogs are not automatons and will inevitably make mistakes, as will the handler, particularly when working at speed. When mistakes occur, don't always blame the dog, rather re-affirm the bonds of mutual love and respect which typify the finest working partnerships.

Remember there's always another day and keep agility fun.

CONVERSION TABLE

6 inches	152mm
7 inches	178mm
12 inches (1 foot)	305mm
15 inches	382mm
18 inches	457mm
20 inches	508mm
24 inches (2 feet)	610mm
3 feet (1 yard)	914mm

1'6" = 1 foot 6 inches = 457mm